To Colleen

Love the Greatest Healer

With love Joy & peace

GERALD O'DOWD

BALBOA
PRESS
A DIVISION OF HAY HOUSE

This book is a work of non-fiction. Unless otherwise noted, the author and the publisher make no explicit guarantees as to the accuracy of the information contained in this book and in some cases, names of people and places have been altered to protect their privacy.

Balboa Press books may be ordered through booksellers or by contacting:

Balboa Press
A Division of Hay House
1663 Liberty Drive
Bloomington, IN 47403
www.balboapress.com
1 (877) 407-4847

Because of the dynamic nature of the Internet, any web addresses or links contained in this book may have changed since publication and may no longer be valid. The views expressed in this work are solely those of the author and do not necessarily reflect the views of the publisher, and the publisher hereby disclaims any responsibility for them.

The author of this book does not dispense medical advice or prescribe the use of any technique as a form of treatment for physical, emotional, or medical problems without the advice of a physician, either directly or indirectly. The intent of the author is only to offer information of a general nature to help you in your quest for emotional and spiritual well-being. In the event you use any of the information in this book for yourself, which is your constitutional right, the author and the publisher assume no responsibility for your actions.

Any people depicted in stock imagery provided by Getty Images are models, and such images are being used for illustrative purposes only. Certain stock imagery © Getty Images.

Print information available on the last page.

ISBN: 978-1-9822-0187-6 (sc)
ISBN: 978-1-9822-0186-9 (hc)
ISBN: 978-1-9822-0190-6 (e)

Library of Congress Control Number: 2018904058

Balboa Press rev. date: 04/10/2018

M Y BIRTH WAS NO ORDINARY delivery, so my mum says. The afterbirth came before me, nearly suffocating me. My mum was put to sleep, so as not to stress her out. She awoke and asked where I was, the doctor gave me to her and that was that. I was born on the twentieth-eighth of October 1963 in my parents' bedroom at 29 Joan Crescent, South East London, a tidy, clean but small, three bedroomed house. My early life is a bit vague; my earliest memory is of when I was around five years old, sitting on my grandad Glynn's knee while he plucked the Christmas turkey. My next memory is seeing my grandad in a coffin at his wake. The lid was off and there he was, white as a sheet, his best friend sat by the coffin talking to him. My mum has confirmed this; it is not my imagination running wild. If you have never heard of a wake, it's an Irish tradition going back decades. The coffin is laid out in the house overnight so family and friends can pay their respects. I wish my grandad had lived longer. He was a good man who was good with his hands, and a poet as well. My mum tells me that he was an intelligent gifted man with great morals. He died aged fifty-two, way too young.

Grandad Glynn was a smoker, which created a severe lung condition, which killed him. Smoking back then was considered cool. Marketing posters and ads made smoking seem sophisticated and debonair, while the reality was early death or a life of addiction. I dislike smoking intensely.

It makes me feel angry that the government won't ban it. People are dying, literally, for a fag which astounds me. Why do we allow young kids to be exposed to it? It's a disgusting habit that needs eradicating from society. My mum nearly died some years back because of smoking. She spent many years recovering from a serious lung condition, like her dad, so I'm pleased to say that she gave up when she came out of hospital and has never looked back. She's now seventy eight and doing great, blessed and grateful for the Lord's help. My mum is a women of great faith, which has helped tremendously over the years.

My childhood was spent playing football most days or climbing trees and investigating the local parks and fields around Eltham, SE9. My best mate was Graham Stack. We used to roam all over the local area, Well Hall Pleasaunce, the farm and the back fields which had football and rugby pitches. We had to climb over a fence, which was no problem to us, and we played in the local allotment and the horses' field, but football was our main concern. We played at every break in school, after school outside Graham's house or my house; we were obsessed and loved playing the game. On a Sunday, all the kids on our estate gathered in the fields on Middle Park Avenue, sometimes up to 30 kids playing, all ages from 7 years old to 15 years old. It was brilliant, there was no time limit; we played until everyone was knackered. Life was great. Sometimes I slept over at Graham's house, which was interesting as they never argued or shouted at each other and it was a loving peaceful house. Our house was loud with lots of shouting arguments and general mayhem. Our house was always busy, my dad was out working all day or in the betting office, my parents argued over money most times. Dad left mum short of money because he lost it on the horses. Of course, they argued over money or my dad's lack of interest in decorating our house. My mum done all the decorating, cleaning, cooking, making us clothes or curtains.

My mum was a real grafter and she never complained. Mum was always trying to make the peace, but Dad was louder and more aggressive than my mum and always had the last word. I heard my mum crying many times but my dad was too macho and hotheaded to care. He went to work and demanded silence when he came home – keep the kids quiet and give me my dinner, He was a product of the times, growing up in the 30s, 40s and 50s. He was born in 1934 and was evacuated as a small child during the Second World War. Dad told me he had a great time learning to read and write with a lovely couple who took good care of him.

My dad was a complicated man; on the one hand, he would help anyone who was in trouble, but would leave my mum crying over money. Dad could be generous to his family or friends but Mum had to struggle. I never saw my parents kiss or cuddle, they showed no affection to each other. One of my dad's sayings was, "I went to school with my belly stuck to my back. You fucking eat your dinner or go to bed hungry." One day, I came home with homework and my dad was home, I asked for some help but Dad just said, "That's what you go to school for, boy." I never asked again. Mum helped with my English when she had the time, but she was busy most of the time so I never bothered asking.

My primary school was Middle Park, just around the corner from our house. I loved it; we could walk to school and back on our own. Life was a mixture of great adventure or noisy uncertainty. We could play outside and roam the local area, we played dare on the railway tracks or went fishing in the Quaggy, a river near the busy A20 dual carriageway. We had no fear, it was all an adventure. We stopped playing on the railway tracks when a kid got killed. My mum was really upset and banned us from going anywhere near them. We never knew the kid but we realised the danger and stopped our stupid behaviour.

The uncertainty at home was confusing, we never knew when Dad would kick off and he would blow his top over the smallest thing. My dad was volatile and could get very angry. My mum would always tell us to be quiet when my dad was home and not to upset him. It was like walking on eggshells. Dad never played with us or cuddled us. He loved us but could not show it. He was a man's man who loved a fight. I'm sure plenty of kids went without affection from their dads. That's life, we knew no difference.

My mate Tyron got hit plenty of times, I saw him get hit a few times so I thought it was normal. My mum did her very best to stop us from getting hit, but sometimes we deserved it. That's why we played out when dad was home; out of sight out of mind. One day Tyron and I climbed up a drain pipe and onto the school roof. It was about 50 feet high, not huge but high enough to get killed. The caretaker caught us and told the headmaster. We got read the riot act, my parents were very angry with me and I was punished and sent to bed early. Also, the school expelled me for a week. I hated being off school and promised never to do it again. We played knock down ginger, where we knocked on strangers doors' and ran away, which pissed them off no end. Another game we played was curb football; we stood either side of the road and tried to hit the curb so the ball came back to you.

One day, me and Graham Stack nicked my mum's fags and went up Eltham High Street to try them out. We hated that experience and we both never did it again. It was disgusting. Why people smoke is a mystery to me, the worst habit ever invented. My mate Tyron had an older brother who used to ride horses bareback. We gathered at the local horses' field to watch him do it. I was in awe of him, he was so brave and cool. He was a good boxer as well. He was also a collector of birds' eggs, he had a massive collection in cases under his bed. I looked up to him. It is not cool today to collect rare eggs or any eggs, but, back then, it was acceptable. One day, Tyron and I decided to climb onto the roof of a derelict house to get pigeon eggs. We were around ten years old. Nowadays, we would be breaking and entering and nicked for our silliness, but, back then, we had no fear, we just did things on impulse. It was a dare and, if you failed, you would be a wally, so we did it. There were holes in the floors, the stairs were broken and rickety – it was a health and safety nightmare. We managed to get onto the roof and collect some pigeon eggs. In hindsight, we were silly fools, but we did it for adventure and devilment. We climbed trees for conkers or just to see how high we could go.

One day, me and Graham found two baby magpies on the ground. We picked them up and took them home. My mum and dad said I couldn't have the bird indoors so I put it in our shed. Sadly, it passed away Overnight. I was devastated. I cried and felt bad for weeks, but Graham's bird survived. He had given the magpie to a lady above Cliff Humphrys' house. The lady fed it through the night and the bird thrived. After a while, the magpie became so friendly. We visited the lady after school to see it. It was the best feeling in the world to see the bird grow strong. After a while, she let the bird fly away into the world. The bird kept returning until, one day, he vanished, never to be seen again. What a lovely lady.

Cliff Humphrys was another good childhood mate. He lived opposite Graham and we all went to the same school. He had a party on his sixth or seven birthday, which I went to good memories. Cliff was a nice kid and a little shy. We all played together, football, climbing and exploring are all fond memories. One day, all the kids were playing football on the green outside our house when a kid called Ted kicked the ball over our fence. He ran to get it. We said, watch out for the dog, but he continued running. When Ted reached our garden, he went inside and came back out, screaming and holding his backside. "Shit, your dog has bit me!" Everyone started laughing and said, "we told you not to go in." It wasn't a deep bite, but it still hurt. We laughed about that for weeks and it still brings a smile to my face today.

My dad loved a van. We had one in our back garden, which Richard and Kevin painted with flowers, so it was a hippy van by the time they had finished. Also, at some point, my dad buried a van in our back garden. He dug a hole and down it went. When lue, our Alsatian dog, died, my dad buried him in the back garden. it was a big garden with chickens, dogs and cats. It was a mess but my dad loved it. lue was more of a guard dog than a pet, but he was ok with us. He let no one near our house he was very protective. When it was raining, my brother David and I played indoors with toy cars and a racing track or with toy soldiers. We were very close in age so we did a lot together. One day, we had a dispute and I threw a toy gun at him, but I missed and hit the front room window, smashing it to pieces. My mum went mad at me and said, "Wait 'til your father gets home," which put the fear of God in me. My mum told my dad it was an accident so I got away without being punished. Good old Mum.

At around 1970, when I was seven years old, some of us kids from the estate played in the church grounds, and someone said the statue of Mary moved, which scared the living daylights out of me. Shit, it kept moving which gave us all the jitters. It went on for weeks until we got bored and found a new thing to occupy us. We played football on the green outside my junior school and, one day, I slid to make a tackle and cut my knee open on a piece of glass. My mate Graham said he could see the bone sticking out, which made me cry. He was over egging it but my mum took me to hospital and I had six stitches. Mum kept me indoors until the stitches came out. I was a right cry-baby. When I was younger, about four years old, I was playing outside our house on the green with my brothers when I flopped lifeless to the ground. All hell broke loose; they thought I was dead and my dad rushed me to hospital, where the doctors discovered I had a high temperature convulsion, my body over heated and shut down. I was back to normal very soon after.

There was always a drama going on … one day, my

brother Kevin got impaled on a spike while trying to climb a railing fence. He slipped and the spike went through his lower mouth. On another occasion, my dad had a fight with a man who chased my brother Richard. The man was really angry, accusing Richard of throwing stuff at him and his dog from the bridge down the road. My dad tried to calm the man down, but he was having none of it. They got into a real fight, punching each other; at one point, the man's dog started biting my dad's legs while the man slashed my dad with the dog's chain. In a moment, my dad picked up the garden fork and pinned the man to our garden fence by his arm. The police arrived and nicked my dad and the man. I am not sure, but I think they both got bound over to keep the peace – who needs Eastenders, ay?

When I was ten, my mum and dad bought me a pair of Puma football boots and a brown leather football for Christmas. I was overjoyed; it was my best present ever and I played football at every opportunity until the boots and ball were worn out.

I loved living in Eltham; my childhood friends, the fact we could explore our surroundings. It was my birth place and playground. We discovered Eltham Palace climbing over the fence and playing in the grounds, swimming every Saturday at the local pool, diving off the diving boards. We had a ball and it was an adventure. My parents let us be free to investigate. We went scrumping apples in the fields, collecting newts, frogs and small fish from the Tarn, the Quaggy and Well Hall Pleasaunce. We had a great time. One year, I went on a council holiday with my brother Richard to Somerset. It was scary being away from home for the first time. It was on that holiday that I learnt how to swim; my brother Richard pushed me in and I swam to the side doggie paddle. Also on that holiday, I fell into stinging nettles and was covered in stings from head to toe. My brother hosed me down with cold water to stop the pain … great experience, not.

Life was good until the age of twelve, when we moved to Shooters Hill, SE18. I was devastated for a long time, believing I had lost all my friends, but in reality, it was only three miles and a bus ride away. We moved school, which was really hard as all my friends were still going to my old school – Graham, Cliff, Tyron and many more. At first, David and I went to Charlton Primary School in Charlton, SE7, for two weeks. I hated every minute of it because we knew no one and I got into a fight during the first week which didn't help our popularity. The class was loud and unruly and my heart sank on the first day and it never stopped hurting for the two weeks we were there. My mum found a school nearer to home called Plumcroft Primary School which, for me, was no better. The headmistress, Mrs Copplestone, who slapped me across the legs for talking, was really strict. I couldn't stand her, she was awful and stern as hell. My class teacher was Mr Anderson, who disliked me intensely. The feeling was mutual and I hated him. The only time I got any praise was when I painted the school stage, my dad donated the paint and I helped paint it.

One day, I was playing football with some lads when the ball went over the fence into some wasteland next to the school. I climbed over to get the ball and stood on a rusty nail sticking out through a piece of wood. The school phoned my mum and she took me to the Brook General Hospital where I had a tetanus injection. It hurt but I got the rest of the week off, brilliant. My concentration was useless; I was always dreaming of playing football, so every break we played. One day, a kid started a fight with me, we grappled and rolled around on the playground floor before a teacher pulled us apart. We got sent to Mrs Copplestone, where we were given a right rollicking. I hated conflict but seemed to get involved in fights on a regular basis. We eventually made friends and, after a while, we settled into our new school.

I played football for the school against other schools on a Saturday morning. My brother David, our friend Tony Quinnel, and other friends, loved playing in our school team in all weather, wind, rain or snow. Life was better after a year or so, we made friends and started investigating the area. One day, David, Tony and I had been to Woolwich Ferry, riding across the Thames several times. As we were walking home, I found an old pram which I thought would make a great go kart. All was well until we got to the Walpole

Estate near Sandy Hill. A gang of kids started shouting at us, telling us to fuck off. We started running, but I was lagging behind because I was pushing the pram. David and Tony got away, but the kids caught up with me and gave me a right Woolwich kicking. They nicked my pram, fucking David and Tony laughed their heads off – fucking wankers. My pride was dented but I lived to tell the tale … I should have ditched the pram and run faster, lol.

It was 1975 and my new friends became great mates: the Vines boys, Sally and Kate, Jill, the Scott sisters, Andy, Neil and Kerry, Ricky, Nicky, Mac. We used to meet after school and hang around the streets or in the local parks, Eaglesfield or Shrewsbury. Me and my brother David played football every Saturday for the school and, on Sundays, for London Boys FC. My mum and dad's best friend, Jimmy, managed London Boys. We won the league and cup, played in tournaments all over, and we went to Belgium for a week, which was our first time abroad. It was fantastic David and I loved it and Jimmy was great. He let us stay up late and he got on stage to sing Elvis songs. The experience was a special one for me and it opened up my mind to happiness. We had a great time, and Jimmy was a fun, open and good man. I was with all my mates and there was nothing better; my memories of that time are precious. I loved playing football with my mates, it was heaven.

David and I made lots of friends and spent a lot of time in

the local youth centres playing football, tennis, swimming, pool, darts, table tennis, badminton, judo. I was never at home. After school, we couldn't wait to get out with our mates. We went scrumping apples, plums and pears. On one occasion, I was up a tree stealing plums, when the owner came out, shouting at us. We all shit ourselves and ran away, but I was still up the tree. As I moved, the branch gave way and I fell out of the tree, I got up and ran, only getting away by the skin of my teeth. The man was really angry, calling us little bastards. We thought it was funny, but in hindsight, I can see how bad it was. Sorry, mister I am really sorry.

It was around 1977 when a gang of us went camping in Kent. It was an adventure into the unknown. About seven of us went by bus to Downe Village, a small place in the middle of nowhere. We walked a few miles in the dark, telling ghost stories, before arriving at the campsite. We put up our tents and sat around telling more gory tales. It was late before we went to sleep, but we never slept well and kept mucking about. We got up early and investigated our surroundings; we went looking for food to eat and found a camp shop that sold sweets, chocolate, crisps and fizzy drinks, so we purchased some goodies and went back to our camp. We stuffed our faces and larked about. The day was okay and we found some workers' machetes stashed in some bushes. We took them back to cut wood for our camp fire and then stole them. The day soon turned into night and we got bored of telling ghost stories. We decided to look for some excitement … we came across the camp shop and thought it would be a good idea to break in. We stole boxes of sweets, chocolate flakes and bottles of fizzy drinks and went back to our camp and stuffed our faces again, making us sick and putting the fear of God in us. What if we get found out? We decided to leave the site at five in the morning; off we trotted, leaving behind all the wrappers from the chocolate flakes and sweets. At some point in our getaway, I decided to put a jar of gob stoppers in my hood. Someone said they heard noise, so we started running and the gob stoppers fell out all over the path. Everyone laughed while running. We reached the village and waited for the bus. After what seemed like a long time, a van pulled up and two very angry men got out. "Get in the van," they said. So we got rumbled … in we got, except for my jammy brother David. He was in a phone box, trying to call home for a lift while the rest of us were taken to a house near to the campsite. The men made us open our bags and sleeping bags, pulling our bounty from within; two of us had hidden the machetes in our sleeping bags so we got well and truly caught red handed. To top it off, a girl standing in a window saw us throwing away evidence into the garden. We were verbally read the riot act and then the police arrived. My fear was my dad … would he hit me for doing this stupid shit? Our parents went ballistic but all I got was a slap around my ears, so I got off lightly. David has never been caught, so he's still on the run from the law, technically!.

Life went on … my school days were spent daydreaming and wishing it would end soon; School was boring; I could not concentrate and the only lessons I liked were English, Art, and Sports. The rest was a waste of time and I got the cane several times for not concentrating and for mucking about in lessons. Mr Spinks gave me six of the best and he really enjoyed it, he skipped before he hit me. I think he was a pervert or something sinister – he looked like one. My headmaster gave me the cane once. He gave me a choice, on the bum or on the hand. I chose the hand, but every time he came down with the cane, I moved my hand. After a few attempts, he went ballistic. "Fucking hold your hand still, O'Dowd."

"Yes, sir," I said, but I still kept moving it, which made him really mad at me. After many attempts, I begrudgingly took my punishment, which was good because my headmaster's eyes nearly popped out of his head with utter rage. My hand was stinging for ages.

Life went on and school was just a place I wanted to get out of, so I started to hop the wage or play truant or bunk off school, whichever you prefer, I would sign the register, then climb the fence and go to a mate's house or hang around the local parks until hometime. I did want to learn but my teachers never had the time to help me. I was so used to switching off and daydreaming that they just thought I was being lazy, which didn't help anyone. If I had more one-to-one tuition, maybe I would have done okay, but I couldn't concentrate at all. School was pointless to me; I never did my homework, my parents were too busy to help, bringing up six kids is tough. My thinking was, get out of school and get a job as quickly as possible, so the day my work experience advisors came to school, I was a little excited, which didn't last long because I had no qualifications and no experience. I left feeling gutted; he literally said that you have no chance in the workplace with no qualifications or experience. I thought, that's ok, I will work for my dad's building company. Sorted, I thought. But, I couldn't leave school for another year, so I continued to not turn up.

One day, my mate Andy Barber said he could get me a job at the Charlton Tyre Centre changing tyres. I jumped at the chance with both hands. Andy had an older brother who worked there; he was good fun and showed us the ropes. I loved it but it only lasted six months because the boss asked me for my P45. "What's that?" I said.

"It's so you can pay tax, son. When you left school, you should have got one." Oh shit, I was still school age.

"Okay," i said. That was that no job for me.

So I started working for my dad. He was okay with me leaving school early, so that's what I did. My dad paid me five quid a day, which was more than I had ever had. I was now a labourer filling skips, pulling down ceilings, general dogsbody. At first, I loved it, but soon my dad decided I should be with him, dropping off materials to the jobs, which I hated. Most of my day was spent sitting outside betting offices in Dulwich, or wherever we were. My dad spent hours in them, studying with diligence which horse to back. In those days, I just did what he said – no grumbling, but I was more bored than my school days. At least I had my mates to banter with back then.

Around 1977, at the age of 14, I met my girlfriend Tracy, who blew my socks off. We fell head over heels in love. She was a year older than me but that meant nothing to us. We spent much time together, as much as possible. We would hang out with our friends Neil and Kerry, Andy, the Scott sisters and Mac, but soon after, we started getting serious and stopped seeing our mates, which, in hindsight, was a bad move. We got totally loved up and enjoyed our own company; we were glued at the hip. When I was around seventeen, we got engaged. My parents loved Tracy like a daughter. We got on really well, but I could not be faithful. Every time I got drunk, I played around. My life revolved around my sporting activities all week, but on the odd night I got free, I was out with my mates, getting drunk and badly chatting up girls – how I ever got laid is a mystery to me as I was useless at the chatting up process. It wasn't very often but I was a cheating shit. Looking back is cringeworthy; I can't believe how insecure I was, so very sad. Getting drunk was the only way I could find the courage to communicate with girls.

Back in 1977, with my friends Mac Neil, Pud, Sally, Kate and Jill, we would meet up at each other's houses and listen to music and chat. This was a fun time and we got on really well, Jill was in love with Andy, Kate liked my brother David who was just finding his feet, I was close to Sally. They were great times, very innocent. Life was really cool, playing football and I had lots of friends – girls and boys.

I started seeing Tracy in 1978 which coincided with my dad losing his business and me getting beat up. I have no clue why it happened, but I found myself at the local youth club, when a kid said he wanted to see me outside. So, before I knew it, he hit me three times on the nose. Another kid jumped in and said, "That's enough." I walked home, crying my eyes out. I was a soft kid who had no idea about fighting. That's when my dad went ballistic; he marched me out of the house and said he wanted me to fight the kid again. I was shitting myself, I couldn't fight my way out of a paper bag, plus he already beaten me up. My dad was really pissed off, but thankfully, we didn't find the kid, but from that moment, on my dad hounded me to join the local boxing club, St. Peters ABC. I was very reluctant but, after a while, my dad said to just go and get fit and it would help with my fitness for football. It made sense, but I never wanted to be a boxer. So, in late 1977, I started going on a Tuesday and Thursday night. I made friends and loved the training, but never wanted to get into the ring. My dad left it a few weeks before he started pressuring me to spar. I felt totally out of my depth but eventually I gave in. Sparring meant hitting your mates, so I was very careful not to hurt anyone, but I got a bloody nose several times. My dad used to get angry with me, "why don't you hit them back, for fuck's sake, son. You're moving well, but you're not hitting back!" I felt perplexed – it was in not my nature to fight, my dad kept nagging me to get tougher in the ring. This went on for a few months, and I was torn between feeling unsure of myself and feeling embarrassed at being a wimp in my dad's eyes. He was so angry with my reluctance to fight.

One night, I was sparring with a mate when my dad got really pissed off. At the end of the round, my dad came to my corner and said to me, "He is taking the piss out of you. Fucking hit him back!" Something changed in me and, in the next round, I started going after the kid. I hit him a few times and he started to back off. My dad was really happy, he was happy all the way home. "See, son, if you let people take the piss, they will. You did good tonight." Because my dad was happy, it made me feel good. Before long, I was taking the sport more seriously, running on my nights off from the gym with the lads, Gerry Level, Rob, Steve Higgins, Lenny, Glen and John. We pushed each other and I was really good at it; in fact, it became my best way of training. I loved running, especially in the rain. It was exhilarating with a sense of freedom.

Gerry Level was a very good runner who won the Gordon's gym marathon back in the day. After about a year of training, sparring and running, I was really fit and my first boxing match was approaching. I was shitting myself but couldn't let my dad down; he was so excited, giving me extra training at home. He perfected my punching when he realised I could punch very hard. He told me to punch while imagining I was punching down a wall. I was very nervous about letting him down, his confidence in me was huge, but I felt more pressure than ever. The days before the bout were worrisome and stressful. I didn't want to do it, but how could I back down now? I would look like a coward. My dad kept going over what I should do, and, when the night came, my first fight was a blur. I was so nervous, but miraculously I won by a majority decision. My dad was over the moon, but I was glad the night was over. On the way home, my dad talked about the fight in detail, mostly about how I *should* have done it. I felt no pride in the victory; in fact, I felt numb. My dad never stopped talking about it, which only put more pressure on me. My next fight was in a church hall in Deptford. My brother David and his girlfriend Jane came to see me fight. Dad was excited but, again, I was so nervous. My time came around and we stepped into the ring. We moved into the centre of the ring, I punched the kid with a jab and, to my amazement, he went down. My first reaction was to pick him up, but the referee pushed me back to my corner and then stopped the fight in my favour. I was shocked at how easy it was but, again, I felt no glory. I was numb, but my dad was so happy. "You stopped him with a jab, son. Now that's power." My trainer, Patsy, was cool about it and we got a running commentary all the way home from my dad. He was overjoyed and very excited. When we got home, my mum took me into the kitchen to ask me if I had really wanted to do it, because I looked so glum for someone who had just won, I felt stupid and told my mum I was okay, but she knew I was only doing it to please my dad. Mum told me I could give up any time I wanted, I continued and Patsy entered me into the schoolboy ABA tournament, which was my third fight and, believe it or not, I won my category, which made my dad's day. I was shocked but, a week later, I boxed against a kid who had won his area title. I lost on a majority decision, which upset my dad as he felt I had won the fight. I wasn't that bothered. After that fight, I boxed all over London and Kent, winning some, losing some, which never bothered me. Win or lose, I never cared that much. I was still playing football, running and swimming, so, for me, boxing was good for the training and banter with the boys, plus I was becoming super fit.

When I played football, I could run for the whole ninety

minutes and extra time too – I was a natural athlete. My team, Hymeed Football Club, won the league and cup, and we went on tour to Holland to play in a tournament. It was great fun from start to finish. Andy, the two Garys, Paul Sims, Micky, Andy Barber – super sub – we had a ball. It was fantastic, the sun never stopped shining, we played in proper stadiums against kids that looked like men, and we met some lovely girls who made the holiday that much better. It was great fun and we really enjoyed the whole experience. Our manager, Buster, was very cool and laidback, a lovely guy. The whole football team loved the tour and I will never forget the lads or the holiday; it was magical with fond memories. My dad came with me, which was ok, but we stayed with different families, which was cool.

After the holiday, my dad's business took a nose dive, and my dad stepped in to save the day and ended up losing all his money on a job. Dad went broke and nearly lost his sanity; his mental health suffered due to the stress and dad was very unpredictable. My mum tried to help my dad by offering to find a counselling therapist, but dad said he wasn't mad, he was angry, but would not seek help.

Life was going badly for our family when my brother George found fame with his band Culture Club, as the colourful front man, Boy George. George came home one Sunday afternoon and played a demo of his songs, I'm Afraid of Me, White Boys and Do You Really Want to Hurt Me, the latter shot to number one all over the world. I was training with my mates at Fisher Amateur Boxing Club when his band Culture Club appeared on Top of the Pops. I said to the boys, "My brother is on Top of the Pops tonight," which they laughed at.

"Yeah …" they said and carried on training.

"No, he really is. Come see." We went down to the youth club underneath our gym, the show started and we waited for Culture Club to come on. The DJ announced them, new on the scene, with their new song, Culture Club's Do You Really Want to Hurt Me. George started singing, his voice was flawless, and my mates asked me if the drummer was my brother … er, no, its the singer. "Fuck off, I fancy her," one of them said.

"Well, that's my brother, lads." The banter went on for weeks. To be fair, the lads were very cool about my brother being gay and no one said anything bad or disrespectful, but they ribbed me tirelessly all in good taste.

My parents were really struggling paying the bills. My mum was trying to run a home on very little money, my dad was fighting for money owed but had little chance of getting back. They left my dad a broken man, skint and out of work. He descended into a dark place, crying, raging and feeling useless. Dad was depressed over his business, he would cry over it, and get angry, which made life hard for my mum and us kids. It felt like walking on egg shells most of the time. I was talking with my mum one day and she started crying. "What can we do?" she said. "Your dad won't get a job, we are sinking fast." My dad was his own boss and found it difficult to ask for a job, but my mum was only earning the living wage working as a cleaner for the local council. I told my mum I would talk to my brother to see if he could help. George stepped up and saved the day. He bought my dad a new car, sent them on a lovely holiday, and helped my mum with all the bills. Seeing my mum happy was great, but my dad was still angry about his business and was still unpredictable with regards to the family – the closer you are, the worse it is.

I started working on building sites over the water in the East End with my brothers Richard and David. I loved it, and I was very happy working during the day and training with my mates at night. One day, George phoned Mum to ask if I would have some photos taken with him. My mum convinced me to do it as I was a bit shy. We did the shoot in Central London and went our different ways, and I thought no more of it, until one day at work, we were all in the hut before starting work, when Big Chris started chuckling. "Take a look at this," he said with laughter on his face. He passed the newspaper around, it came to me and I was really shocked.

"Fucking hell," I said … there I was, a massive photo of me and George in the centre pages of the Sun newspaper.

All the lads kept taking the piss all day – in fact, for weeks. I was shocked and a little nervous; it was all too much for me.

I liked running so I entered the local marathon from Plumstead to Chatham in Kent. No-one knew about my brother on the run, which was cool with me, as i could do without the attention. My mum and dad came along to see me do it, which was great. My mum bought me a gold chain with a boxing glove on it. I was over the moon to finish my first marathon; I was never bothered about winning, for me taking part with my mates was good enough and I took satisfaction from it. That's why I was never going to be a champion boxer; I never had the desire to be one. Unfortunately, my dad was convinced otherwise, and it made him happy, so I kept up the pretence with a heavy heart.

One day my mate Neil Wilson said he was going traveling to Germany, India, and Greece, and asked if I wanted to go with him. "Too right," I said, but I knew my dad would be angry. My mum was happy but nervous; I was nervous too but I felt it would be great fun. My dad hated the idea and stopped talking to me. He was livid. Neil's mum paid for my ticket. On the day I left, my dad screamed obscenities at me, saying I was stupid, swearing, saying he had wasted all his time on me, for me to give it all up was fucking disrespectful. I left the house in tears, with my mum feeling sad, but glad I got out. Germany was great fun. I was very shy, which made it difficult for me. but everyone was really friendly and kind

So, after a few weeks, I settled in and we found some work in a supermarket. All we had to do was fill the shopping bags and sometimes walk the shopping to the shopper's car – easy work but we got tips which kept us in beer money. We played football, went running, swimming played basketball, and, most nights, we went drinking which was good fun. Neil and I got plastered on our first night which set the tone for our stay in Germany.

Neil's sister Kerry was working in a hotel and looked out for us, introducing us to all her friends; she was really cool and lovely. We met a girl called Maxine, who let us stay in her digs. I fancied her and she fancied me, but we never got it on because I was so shy. She was pretty and good fun while I was feeling a little homesick and out of my depth. We stayed two months and had some great times. One day, two guys stripped naked and skied down the slopes, which was hilarious. We went drinking a lot and did a lot of sport. After six weeks, I decided to phone home. My mum answered and it was good to hear her voice. We chatted about everything, including my ex-girlfriend, who had been visiting my parents on a regular basis. Mum said she had lost a lot of weight and was really sad we had split up. When I got off the phone I told everyone I was going home. Two weeks later, I arrived home with a full beard, long hair and a bag of dirty washing. If I am honest, I was glad to see my family and my friends. Tracy and I got back together, which pleased my parents, and Neil went off to India with Greg for a few months, then onto Greece for the summer. They had a ball while I got back into working as a general dogsbody on building sites around London.

I continued my football, boxing and marathon running. I used to run to work and back, or cycle there and back. And my brother George was doing amazing things with his career, singing with Luther Vandross, Stevie Wonder, Diana Ross … you name it, he did it. He made guest appearances on chat shows all over the world. Culture Club and my brother Boy George went massive in most countries; they had massive hits but the press never left him alone. If he blew his nose, it was front page news. Fame comes at a cost. You become media fodder and open to scrutiny, private and personal. As a family, we were proud of my brother's achievements, but the press never left him alone or us.

In 1984, after running several marathons and triathlons, I entered the Fosters Quadrathon, the toughest race in the world. I was twenty years old and very gung-ho. My dad told me not to do it but that made me more determined. In hindsight, he was right; I was much too young for that kind of endurance race. I started my training with gusto and the media were very interested in my participating in the race. I featured in the Sun, the Daily Star, and other publications. If I am honest, the media was a thorn in my side, which made me wary and apprehensive, which, in turn, put pressure and stress on me that I didn't need. We featured on London Tonight and in all the local newspapers in my area. My brother George was riding high at this time with Culture Club, and the media loved my brother – he was talented, colourful and funny. They loved the idea that George wore make-up and I was an ordinary lad who loved sports. They described us as being worlds apart, but that was just their way of making the stories more interesting. George was described as a gender bender, and me as a macho sports fanatic, two very different people, but the reality is that we were both talented in our own chosen fields. Looking back, the media used the differences to maximum effect. I looked up to my brother and was very proud of his success, but I hated the media intrusion. They made up stories most of the time. I was doing things I loved to do and was no different from my brother really.

The family became very well known in South East London and my training was going well for the Quadrathon. The race consisted of a two mile sea swim, fifty kilometer race walk, a hundred mile cycle race and then a full 26.2 marathon race run. The local press were cool – they covered our efforts with correct facts. My mates, Paul and Mick, and I helped local charities raise money, and we helped to raise money and awareness for the first residential home for eight physically and mentally impaired adults, Project 28, which was launched in 1984. Paul, Mick and I supported

around twenty five miles when someone told us we have one mile to go. Great, we thought. But they were wrong; it was the twenty third mile and we had three miles to go, which felt like a mountain to climb, but we got through it and continued to the finish line. When I saw the finish line, I felt elated and happy. The joy of having a massage and shower was fantastic. After all the interviews, my dad drove me home, I went to bed and slept 'til the afternoon of the next day. I was physically spent and the elation I felt when I finished the race was gone. My dad went to the local shop to buy the newspapers which had front page photos of me finishing and crossing the line. One said i was a super man and other headlines said silly rubbish that I felt was over the top. I should have felt elated and happy but I felt low and depressed. I was all over the local press, which should have made me feel proud, but I felt so low and not that interested. After a few days off, I went back to work for my friend Johnny, which was a delight. The lads took the piss out of me because I had no energy to do anything; I was physically and mentally spent, my desire and passion was at a low point, and I felt detached and dull because the race and training was over.

Work felt like a chore so I started drinking with my mates, which made life interesting again. We partied all over London – in the East End, Camden Palace, Lime Light, Central London, South London, West London, North

London and all over Kent. I worked as a hod carrier for my mate Johnny, which was hard work but good fun. We went drinking every weekend, during our dinner break and after work. Johnny was a crazy madman but very funny. We got into scraps, but only silly drunken stuff, nothing too heavy. Drinking became my best friend. That is, until my twenty first birthday. The night was going along okay, when a guy I didn't know offered me a line of cocaine. I had never touched drugs, but I was drunk and feeling insecure and self-conscious, so I said, "Show me what to do." He did and I sniffed my first ever line of cocaine, which felt amazing. That night, I became addicted to coke. I loved the feeling and buzz, and every weekend was spent drinking and sniffing. I only saw my girlfriend in the week, but only a few nights as I was still training more than the average person: running, gym work, boxing training, football … in my mind, I had no problem. Life was good, or so I thought. The truth was that I felt useless and unhappy. Underneath the drinking and drug taking, I felt lost. Everyone thought I was a happy chap having a good time but, beneath the mask, I was a confused, unsure young man, trying to live up to my superman persona. I wasn't happy in my relationship with my childhood sweetheart, but I didn't have the guts to end it.

My life was unhappy because I was living a lie. People thought I was a tough party animal, but, in honesty, I was being someone I was not. While drinking and taking drugs,

I gave off the persona of I don't care, lets party. I had one night stands that made me feel like shit the next day. I hated myself for cheating but the drink and drugs numbed my mind and feelings. One day, walking through Woolwich town centre, I bumped into my childhood friend's mum, Mrs Stack. I was so pleased to see her. "How are you?" I said with a big smile.

She looked down and troubled. "You don't know, Gerald?"

"What?" I replied.

"It's Graham. He is dead." I was shocked to my core.

"No," I said, "it can't be true."

But she said, "Yes, it is true, Gerald." I was so sad and confused. Graham was a nice guy who had just became a father for the first time and had everything to live for. I felt tears coming so I asked when he was being buried. We chatted for a while then I left and went straight to the pub and got drunk. I remember waking up the next day thinking it was a nightmare and that it was just a bad dream, but I called Mrs Stack who gave me the time and date of Graham's funeral. The last time I saw Graham, he was excited about his new baby. What the fuck had happened? I held my emotions together during his funeral, but just went on a massive bender for weeks after.

My attitude changed towards life. I thought, *fuck it, life is shit.* Graham's death had a negative effect on me. When my aunty killed herself, I was really hurting but could not express my feelings. Then my uncle died aged 42 from alcohol abuse and life seemed so unfair. I thought, *fuck it,* and started partying again, I started to not care about anything. Life was shit and that was that, my life spiralled out of control, alcohol and cocaine most days. I was angry and resentful, which started to make me ugly and paranoid. My life became complicated and difficult, the drink and drugs patched up the gaping holes in my life. It covered the monumental flaws in my character, and people around me could see my uncaring attitude, I must have been a horrible person back then. My moral compass was off target; I was sleeping around, fighting and being a complete prat. I was charged with drink driving twice and told that, if it happened again, I would go to prison.

One night, while high on cocaine and alcohol, I smashed up my girlfriend's car. It was a write-off, but, worse still, I nearly killed a mate. My life was a car crash and, by 1986, I was being a foolish dickhead with no direction. I was getting a reputation for fighting and for being a womaniser. One day, me and a mate of mine were building a wall in my mum's back garden and, while working on the wall, we drank a bottle of whisky. The wall was pissed and so were we. When we finished the wall, we decided to walk to the pub. While there, my bad behaviour got us thrown out so we carried on walking towards Woolwich. It was my drinking that got us into trouble; all I can do is apologise for my bad behaviour. I am ashamed of myself for acting this way. I was a loose cannon, behaving in a wrong manner, but, because I kept myself fit, I was under the illusion that I was okay – what a fool I was.

Soon I was starting to get paranoid when doing cocaine, but I never stopped. I hated my life and felt disillusioned. With no direction or focus, I was lost in drunken stupidity and a cocaine paranoid haze. I stopped going out and promised my girlfriend I would stop my negative ways. As a couple, we got on really well and never argued or had bad feelings towards each other. I got really fit and stayed home, which worked a treat. Life was good, we were very happy. Without drink or drugs in my life, I was an angel, a nice person, but I was insecure and felt not good enough. At my core, I was a good guy but I had no purpose or passion. My job never changed – I was a low paid dogsbody with no aspirations.

My mum had always told me to read but I could not concentrate long enough. My desire was to change but I had no vision or no imagination. Sports kept me fit, and that was my salvation. I am certain the exercise helped me a lot and kept me sane; it was the reason I could keep on a level playing field. Being a sports fanatic boxer, whose brother was a megastar, was a major factor why the media reported on all my indiscretions. Having a famous name was a tag that was a heavy cross. In hindsight, it was the drugs that caused my problems, not my brother's fame. One Saturday, a tabloid newspaper ran a centre page assassination on my family, describing the family as dysfunctional and nuts. I was described as a thick idiot who was the most stupid of all, which, if I am honest, was embarrassing and cringeworthy. I felt ashamed of myself. I laughed it off but it hurt like crazy, and my self-esteem sunk lower than ever before.

One afternoon in 1987, one of my mate's called on me, honking his car horn from downstairs and shouting my name, I came down the stairs, telling him to stop making so much noise. "Gerry, you have got to try one of these." "What the fuck are they?"

"E, mate. Ecstasy. They are fucking brilliant. The best buzz you have ever had, mate." I said I would see him Friday night, but had no intention of trying one. We went to the Camden Palace and had a few pints, which loosened me up. We got talking and my mate handed me my first E. I popped it in my mouth and waited for it to work. After about fifteen minutes, I said that they must be duff as nothing was happening … just as I said that, it kicked in. The feeling was euphoric and like nothing I had ever had before. My life changed that night. Within a week, I stopped drinking beer and started using Ecstasy. It was a revelation. Every weekend, I was going up the Camden Palace, dropping E, dancing all night. It was a love drug and my whole demeanour changed.

I hugged everyone, loving the buzz and loving the vibe; it was amazing. By the summer of 1987, I was well into the emerging dance scene, growing my hair and feeling excited about life. It was great fun. In the month of July 1987, I went off to Ibiza. We went to Amnesia and partied 'til 6am, watching the sun rise while buzzing off my nut. My communication skills were useless and I had nothing interesting to say. I was an airhead with space to rent. We partied all night in Amnesia 'til dawn then went off to a club called Space 'til about 2pm. Then we slept 'til whenever, then started all over again the next night. In hindsight, I must have been dull company but I believed in the love side of the scene and also thought everyone was enjoying the drug and feeling the loved up experience. Again, in hindsight, not everyone was doing E. People were onto the fact that there was good money to be made. I was oblivious to this as I was enjoying the drugs too much. My only concern was getting high and loved up. These pills could change the world, I believed. After two weeks, it was time to go home. Looking back on that holiday, I am amazed that I am still alive as we drove motorbikes all over the place while high on E.

It was a small scene which I believed was peaceful and inclusive, but not everyone was loved up. Cunning people, seeing how lucrative this scene could be, started to get involved. When I got home, I started to go to Spectrum, under the arches at Charing Cross train station, which is now

Heaven. The vibe was cool and all the people were more or less peaceful. I was downing E with no regard for my body health or my mind ... reckless tomfoolery. I had no clue as to what my mind was going through; I never gave it a thought. I do not know what people thought about me as I was too busy getting high. The music was perfect harmony to E; the two went together perfectly. House music, lots of water, dropping E ... it was an amazing buzz and harmless scene, which, looking back, was not the case.

One day, this guy introduced himself to me. We chatted a little and I trusted him implicitly – I had no reason not to. He was funny and very cool. He drove a red sports car, which he borrowed from his boss. He was a good looking, intelligent guy who loved E as much as me. I introduced him to my family and girlfriend, and we became good friends, or so I believed.

I have always done sports and exercise, which I believe helped my mental state, even though I ended up in a psychiatric secure mental health hospital, diagnosed with schizophrenia. My body took a battering but my mind took a monumental battering. I never for one minute believed I would become so paranoid that I truly believed my family wanted me dead.

My new friend and I talked about doing some club nights, which started really well. We did our first night in a small warehouse in Kennington, South London. We never made a lot of money, but it was never my intention to make money – it was all about the music and buzz. I loved the feeling E gave me. It made me feel loving and it also made me feel part of a movement. Little did I know about human nature. The people who saw the money to be made went in for the kill. I fell in love with the music, which still makes me feel nostalgic, and Kennington was a huge success in terms of a great night. There must have been three hundred plus people coming through the doors. It was a small venue and people had a great time. I loved it. The next venue was a nightclub in Leicester Square, bang in Central London. We made banners to go around the dancefloor, and the club had really good lighting and a great sound system. Again, I made no money but it never bothered me. The night was another success in terms of people having a great night. I was no business man, nor was I a money man. My philosophy was pure and simple: if people had a great night, I was happy. We did a night at my brother Kevin's mate's club in Greek Street, not far from Leicester Square. It was another success, another great night, but, after that night, we stopped. Again, we made no money so we made the decision to stop.

Our love of clubbing carried on, going to Sunrise, Biology, Rage, Spectrum, the Clink in London Bridge and other warehouse raves all over the country. There were better business men than us putting on great nights. It was more fun for me going to other places – no pressure, no stress. We got asked to do a night at the Tunnel Club in Greenwich, which, again, turned out to be a money loss for us. Another great night with nothing to show for it. We were useless business men, but, again, it never bothered me too much. Life was good, the scene was going from strength to strength and everything seemed good.

I was still doing some fitness work from time to time and believed I was in an okay condition. How dangerous for me to be taking E pills and still working out. Madness playing with fire, stupidity in hindsight. My girlfriend was pregnant and soon I was going to be a dad. What the fuck was I playing at? But, because I felt in control, I felt I was doing okay. I was deluded and thick to think that way. One day, I decided to give up the drugs and get fit again, which lasted a few months. I missed the buzz and feeling off my head because I was addicted to the drug and the feelings it gave me. My son was born in January 1989, and I stopped going out for a while, but had no determination mentally to stop, even though I was a dad, which I am ashamed of. I kept taking drugs and was easily tempted back into a life of debauchery. I was a dumb airhead who couldn't communicate on a normal level. Drugs became my way of being in the world. If I was off my tits, I didn't need to be normal. My mindset was out of touch with reality and the drugs became more important than anything. I was starting to get jaded and was tempted back into doing a rave. I told myself I was doing it for my girlfriend and child, which gave me the motivation to do it. It turned out to be another disaster for me. I made no money and ended up in court, charged with being the main organiser, which was far from the truth. The court case was a shocking wake up call for me and made me realise I had no friends in this scene. The case was over in a few days, I was found not guilty and no one else was mentioned in the case. This should have stopped me from going out and doing drugs. My girlfriend kicked me out and my mates kept calling for me to go clubbing, I was lost in a sea of confusion, and addicted to punishment, my mind started to feel anxious and paranoid but I could not stop taking drugs. One night, not long after the rave, my mate convinced me to take an LSD trip, which fucked me up big time. He said it would make me feel better about things, but I just fell into a dark paranoid hell. He must have known I would have a nightmare.

My life started to fall apart at the seams from that moment on. He was my friend and I trusted him, but, in hindsight, he was never a true friend, because he left me in deep paranoia. A few weeks later, he convinced me to go to Glastonbury with some of his friends. He said they were good people, and I believed him and trusted him. Driving to the festival, they offered me a drink of water which was spiked with LSD. By the time we got there, I was in a paranoid hell. I was very confused and feeling very uncertain. My friend had betrayed me and was laughing at me. At some point, two guys started grilling me about my brother George but I was so paranoid I could not talk. After what seemed like a lifetime, I plucked up the courage to leave. I walked to the train station feeling absolutely terrified and alone, tripping out of my mind.

The station master put me in a room and locked it for me. He saved my life that night as I was prepared to kill myself by throwing myself into the train's path. It was Saturday night and all the trains had stopped for the night, and by the time the next one was due, the trip had calmed down somewhat, but I was feeling very paranoid and self-conscious. Everyone seemed to be looking at me, knowing what was going on. It was the worst feeling ever. My mind started to play tricks on me and everyone was in on the plot.

My so-called friend called me to ask if I wanted to take part in a TV programme about the rave scene, which turned out to be a nightmare. I was hood winked into talking about one person, but I never said anything about him. I was asked if he was the main organiser of a rave, to which I replied, "No." That's all I said. I was being set up by the journalist and my so-called mates; they knew the truth, but it was made to look like I was the bad one. After that programme, my life was in serious danger, even though I never said anything to incriminate anyone and all the people involved knew I was innocent.

Sporting achievements

London boy's football club	1973-1974	Won league and cup
Hymead football club	1979-1980	Won league and cup
St Peters amateur boxing club	1978-1982	Won 10 lost 5 fights
Fisher amateur boxing club	1982-1984	Won 6 lost 4 fights
Eltham amateur boxing club	1985-1987	Won 4 lost 1 fight
Turned Professional	1990-1991	Lost first fight
Run 1st Marathon	1981-	2 hours 56 min
Run 2nd Marathon	1982-	3 hours 5 min
Run 3rd Marathon	1983-	2 hours 45 min
Quadrathon	1984-	20 hours 36 min
Swim 2 miles in sea Walk 30 miles Cycle 120 miles Run 26 miles		
Iron Man Triathlon	1985-	11 hours 48 min
Swim 2 miles Cycle 120 miles Run 26 miles		
London Triathlon	1984-	3 hours 5 min
Swim 1 mile Cycle 14 miles Run 7 miles		
London Triathlon	1985-	2 hours 59 min
Run 5 Marathons between	1981-1986	Total 10 Marathons
Run 12 half Marathons	1981-1986	Total 12 half Marathons

—

My life became intolerable and suicide became my only option. I told my ex-girlfriend that I didn't say anything. but she said I was a fool to even talk to them. My life became a living hell. I started to believe I was being followed because my mind was so paranoid; I believed my family hated me, my so-called friends stopped calling me. life was a living hell, After a few months, I started to go back to the gym, I started to feel a little better and I joined Eltham boxing club. It was great to be back with my mates – my real mates – feeling good again. The drugs were a curse to me, and the people involved with drugs are unfeeling and don't care for anyone but themselves and the money; they are ruthless.

Boxing, training and running were a life saver for me. I was getting better and fitter by the day, my girlfriend let me back into her life and gave me another chance, I was working on building sites again and starting to enjoy life with my son. We went on three holidays in one year – Cornwall, Ireland and Euro Disney. Life seemed to be going the right way for once. My mate Mick started a big job on Marlborough House in Pall Mall, Central London, opposite St James' Park. It was a great job; I was working with Johnny, Peter, Red, Dan, Mad Dog Dooner, Jim the Hod and Big Gus. We had a ball. Gus is the funniest man I have ever worked with. If we worked the weekend, we would finish at around one in the afternoon and then spend the rest of the day in the pub. Jim would sing Sweet Caroline and other great tunes. I was in a good place mentally and starting to enjoy life again.

In 1990, I turned professional boxer with Bob Paget thinking I could maybe reach British title level. My first professional fight was at the London Arena in Docklands, East London. I was first on the bill, which big George Foreman was headlining. I got very fit and boxed at light middleweight. My opponent was a journeyman with ten fights under his belt. I was rusty in terms of my confidence but I was determined to give it a go in order for my son to have a decent life. my intention was pure and honest. On the night of the fight, I was really nervous about fighting in front of five thousand people in the London arena. As I entered the ring, my trainer Bob said it was being televised coast to coast across America, which added more pressure. The fight went six rounds and I lost on a majority result. I may have lost the fight but felt some pride getting myself out of the gutter of drug life and into a decent shape – it felt good to be fit again and drug free.

I was enjoying life again with my mates Mick, Johnny, Gus and all the boys who I worked with. I decided to give up boxing and concentrate on my family life. My mate Ricky was my running partner, and we ran most nights, in all kinds of weather. At weekends, we ran full and half marathons and triathlons. My mental state was good, life was better without drugs, and my son was my inspiration now. I would bathe him, read him stories, take him to the play parks, go swimming. We were really close. My girlfriend was angry with me but wanted to give us a good go, so I settled back into a normal life – whatever normal is. I was born into a dysfunctional family, so normal means nothing. I was doing my very best to lead a decent life with my son and girlfriend.

After a little while, on a night out, my drink was spiked with LSD again. My mind became intensely paranoid. I didn't talk at all and just stared into space, nodding when appropriate. When I got back home, I pinned the curtains in my bedroom to the window frame and lay clothes across the bottom of the door to stop the light getting in. No one knew about my ordeal; I told no one. My family was oblivious to my mental state, and I spent the day in my bedroom, feeling strange, anxious, paranoid and utterly lost. At some point in the evening, I went to sleep but woke up a few hours later at around 2am. My mind was still feeling strange, like I was going mad. Was I losing my mind? I thought dark thoughts of suicide and death and I wanted the mad thoughts to stop but they lasted forever. A few days went by before I went out of the house. I went to B&Q and bought a can of black emulsion paint, then went home and painted my bedroom totally black – walls, ceiling, door and all the woodwork, with the curtains being pinned to the window frame, which kept all the light out. My behaviour was erratic; I thought people were following me and that my family hated me.

One night, I was in my room crying when I heard people talking outside. I believed they were waiting for me to go out so they could kill me. My mum knocked on my bedroom door, "Are you alright, Gerald?" she said.

I opened the door and said, "No, there are people outside, waiting to kill me." She went to the window and looked through the crack in the centre of the curtains.

"There is no one there, son." But I was crying and terrified. Mum tried to comfort me but I curled up in a ball in the corner of the room and cried my eyes out. My mum kept coming to my room to check on me until I went to bed. The next day, I decided to go for a run. I was nervous, paranoid and very anxious but convinced myself to go out and run. I got to the bottom of the hill, by a telephone box, and ran into the road. I thought I saw a man with a gun and panicked. My heart jumped out of my chest. I run home and told my mum; she was calm and said I must be seeing things but I was sure he was trying to kill me.

My mum was worried sick about me and asked my dad to stay with me while she went to work, which he did. One evening, I was in our kitchen with my mum, sister and other family members when I decided to go and kill myself. I went into the back garden and cut some hose pipe, threw it over the fence and walked back indoors. No one batted an eyelid. On my way out of the house, I picked up my sister's car keys, walked out, picked up the hose pipe and then drove to Woolwich Common. I put the pipe in the exhaust, taped around it, then put it through the car window. I sat down in the car and turned on the engine. After a while, I felt sleepy but caught my eyes in the mirror. I saw my sister crying, which made me open the car door. I couldn't go through with it. I fell out of the car crying ... no one knew what I was up to. After a short while, I drove back home. When I was parking the car, my mate Neil pulled into the close. I was crying and he was trying to comfort me when my dad walked around the corner. I told Neil not to say anything, he kept his word, my dad was kind to me but I couldn't tell him why I was crying, and we walked into the house and had a cup of tea, Neil stayed a while before leaving and I went to my room with my family oblivious to my attempted suicide. During the next few months, I went to my doctor to ask for help. He sent me to see a psychiatrist at the local hospital. She was old and never once asked me a question about me. All she talked about was my brother George. I left, never to return; a total waste of time. No one seemed to know how to help me. In no way am I blaming anyone for my mental health problems, and I hold my brother George in the highest regard, and no one is to blame but me for my life experience; in fact, my brother tried to help me by letting me stay at his house in Hampstead, North London.

While I was there, he got me into a therapy centre. I was suffering from paranoid psychosis, which the centre had no experience of. I had acupuncture, music therapy and counselling, which helped a little, but I needed psychiatric help and medication. One day, I was cycling to the rehab when I spotted a guy on a mobile phone. A few hundred yards away another man was chatting on a mobile phone. I started to think I was being followed and these guys knew each other. I turned around and went back to my brother's house. I was constantly looking out of the windows to see if anyone had followed me.

That evening, there was a guy standing outside the house with a gun. I was shitting myself and was very anxious and frightened. My mind was in constant turmoil. Paranoia is hell. My brother George let me stay for a few months, which I am grateful for. We did meditation and exercise, which helped me a little. I went back home and signed up for a social science access course at Woolwich College. The course was challenging and tested my mental resolve. I trusted no one and made no lasting friendships, but lasted the academic year, finishing in July 1994.

In late 1993, I was given a gift from my brother George. He had got involved with an organisation called Turning Point, which runs groups on personal development. I was up for anything that would help my mental state. On the first evening of the course, Graham Brown, the course leader, talked about going back to the beginning of our conception, to a time before we were born, where we chose this life time and all our experiences. I found the course heavy going and extremely deep and felt completely out of my depth. Everyone was nice but I was a labourer from Woolwich, South East London, and nearly everyone else was middle class, well-educated and clever. I was skint, uneducated, out of work and paranoid. I tried to take onboard the philosophy and teaching, but found the course very challenging and a bit far out.

The course would start at 10am. It went on all day and into the night, sometimes until 3am, with few breaks. Part of the course was to break down all the barriers which makes the person more open to what was being said, which didn't do it for me. I was way too busy thinking about how everyone was way too clever, my nerves were tense, I felt anxious and way out of my comfort zone. It was deep beyond my level of understanding at that time and was more advanced than anything I had ever done. It was my first meditation experience, which I loved. The meditation helped me a lot but I still could not talk within our small groups or within the whole group. I was trapped in my head, feeling like an idiot lost in isolation. I was going through the motions and made some progress but I felt separate from the group and teachers.

As I say, the people and teachers were kind and lovely but I felt totally Insecure. The course was intense, which created a deep fear in me. I could not wait for the course to finish so I could go home where I felt comfortable locked in my bedroom. I was not ready for this course at that particular time; my mental state was not right. I met a girl called Fiona on the course and spent a few months in a relationship with her. It was lovely and we did fall for each other, but our worlds were so different. She was an editor for a successful magazine, and I was skint and had no prospects. I thought it was never going to work, plus my mental state was bad and getting worse at times. Living with mental health is challenging enough without other stress on top. I fell in love, but felt the differences in our lives were too great for us to last. It was all in my head, thinking I was not good enough or intelligent enough.

Fiona was lovely and is now married with two children, so all's well that ends well. Our time together was good and lovely, and I have fond memories of Fiona. After a short while, my mental health started to get worse, so I was advised to go to Turning Point again, which I did without hesitation. Not once was I advised to see a qualified therapist or counsellor. It cost a fortune to do the course and counselling as it was £50 an hour, which I could not afford. I had one session with one of the teachers but it didn't help my mental health. I signed up again to do Turning Point; again, I felt that I was not good enough or intelligent enough. The course was very deep and I did not get it.

On my course, I met a lady called Karen who was doing

the course so she could live to see her two children grow up and to be with her husband for life. Karen and I talked a lot and I could feel her pain and anxiety. She was a beautiful soul. Karen was diagnosed with cancer and was doing Turning Point in the hope of curing the horrible disease. Graham, the course leader, said she needed to know that we choose our life experiences before we come here, which now still feels harsh. Karen was desperate for a cure, but the reality was she had no chance. When I was in Ireland helping as a course helper, we got the news she had passed away. I was devastated and truly shocked, but people said that she had chosen it. I was confused and could not understand the lack of empathy. It was said very matter of fact – life goes on, they said. My confidence was shaken to the core. How would I be healed? Did I choose my mental health issues? My life seemed bleak after Karen's death and I was just going through the motions and lost focus. Then, one evening during my second Turning Point course, I got talking to Gilly Malone, who was lovely. We got on really well and chatted for a while. We were put into different groups that evening and, at the end of the night, we got talking again and ended up staying at the same house – another course member put us up because we had to start really early in the morning. After the course, we exchanged phone numbers.

Gilly was close to a guy called Ian from the same course and they spent a few weekends together afterwards. Gilly and I talked quite a bit, but not romantically, and I genuinely thought she was a friend and that she and Ian were an item. A few weeks went by, and Gilly called me and said that Ian needed us to go see him. "Okay," I said, "no problem."

Gilly picked me up that evening and we drove to his flat in Kennington. Ian lived on the top floor of a tower block. We went up and got talking and, at some point, Ian said he needed a bath. He asked me to go into the bathroom with him and told me that Gilly really liked me. "I thought you guys were in a relationship?" I said.

"No," he said. "She likes you."

We talked while Ian was having a bath and had a cuddle.

Gilly was kind lovely and beautiful. I fell in love instantly. We got very close in no time at all. We fell in love, deep love, and six weeks into our romance we decided to get married. Everyone was shell shocked and my family were worried because they believed I was not in the right frame of mind. Gilly's family could not believe it and everyone thought we were crazy, but on the 27th August 1994, we got married – Mr and Mrs O'Dowd. We were very happy, but my mental demons kept raising their ugly head … fear, anxiety and paranoia. On the surface, we were happy but I was deeply scared and felt inadequate, isolated and not good enough. I felt Gilly was wasting her time with me. I had no qualifications, no money and no confidence in myself. I was frightened of my own shadow. My ability to run marathons, do triathlons, box, was gone. My mind was weak and I felt useless. We moved into Gilly's house that she had lived in with her ex-partner; that felt very uncomfortable. I met him soon after we got together – he was a nice guy and I liked him.

We helped on many Turning Point courses, making tea, putting together the rooms for the course, decorating with flowers. I put 100% into helping in every situation I could. On one course, I met a guy called Graham who was a musician. We got on okay and met a few times to jam. We talked about doing some gigs on Turning Point courses. A few weeks went by and Graham started to get unwell and ended up in a psychiatric hospital. I was shocked but, again, he got no help from Turning Point. Gilly and I went to see him and he was on a locked ward, crying and going through a tough time mentally. He couldn't talk to me because he was in a bad way. We asked the nurse if we could give him some toiletries and multivitamins, along with some fresh fruit. She said it was okay and we left after a while, feeling very low. "What the fuck happened to him?" I kept saying. Gilly was shocked at seeing Graham like that, but Turning Point said he must have asked for it on a spiritual level, which I could not get my head around. A few days later, we went back to see Graham. He was still crying and very confused, but the nurse said we could take him for a walk around the hospital. We did take him and I tried to talk to him but he was crying and made no sense. We left him that night in a mess and we never went back. A lady from Turning Point kept in touch with Graham after he left the hospital. A few weeks later, she told me he was doing okay, but I never found out the reason why he ended up there.

While on a course helping, a lady said her partner committed suicide after attending Turning point, which the main teacher said was sad but he would have done it anyway and then just carried on with the course. I was feeling very paranoid about my mental health because I couldn't talk about it. One day, I summoned up the courage to talk to a teacher, but she said I was having a bad day and not to worry, leaving me feeling stupid for asking. Gilly was sure I needed to do something to fill up my time, so I signed up for a college course at Aylesbury College, close to where Gilly worked. The course was a sports therapy diploma and was five days a week, which did help me from thinking too much about anything else. At break times, I had no one to talk to so met Gilly for lunch at her workplace most days. I became friendly with one lad and he came to my home a few times, but he never kept in touch after the course. Most days, I was on my own; everyone was polite but never asked for my phone number or to meet up after school. In hindsight, it must have been the way I was with them. My paranoia would not go away, however hard I tried. Meditating, swimming and going to the gym was not working for me, so Gilly and I decided I should do Turning Point again, which I did willingly, without hesitation. Anything to help with my mental state. My dad was on the course helping, which did not help my situation. I felt my dad and Gilly being there added pressure and stress; I could not open up and I felt restricted and paranoid.

After the course, my family asked to see Gilly privately. My mum, brother and his wife met at my brother's house in Luton, not too far away from where we lived in Tring. She went along, but felt I was not standing on my own two feet and being honest with myself. She felt that I needed to get a grip and be a man. My family told Gilly that I needed help, but by now Turning Point was number one priority and the answer to everything. We both felt I could get well with love and Turning Point. We went to Ireland to help on a course and had our first and only fall out; we argued over Gilly's commitment and blinkered view that Turning Point was the answer. She stormed off for a while before returning in an angry mood. We slept and made up the next morning. I felt trapped and isolated in my mind and no one understood me, especially Turning Point.

In our time together, I left several times, going back to my parents' house in South London. Each time I left, we talked over the phone and always ended up getting back together again. One day, I left for good, but this time I meant it. Turning Point was not the magic cure. I do not blame anyone for my mental health problems, especially Gilly or anyone at Turning Point, but I created the problem by taking too many drugs. I needed psychiatric support not new age thinking; I was paranoid, not lazy or unfriendly. Paranoia was my curse.

Gilly and I talked again on the phone but I did not want to go back. The next time I saw Gilly was when she came to my parents' house with Nigel, a member of Turning Point and a close friend of Gilly's. We talked for a while and Nigel asked me if I loved Gilly.

"Yes, I do, but I can't get her to listen to me. My head is not right," I said. We talked about a few things before I made the decision to go back with them. My mum asked Nigel to look after me, which he said he would.

One day, when I was at Nigel's house, we were talking about my lack of commitment and my flaky mind and attitude towards my relationship with Gilly. He said he had a lady friend who regularly spent time in a mental health hospital because she did not want to be in the real world and she was choosing to live that life. The conversation made me feel stupid as I could not get the Turning Point message; after all, Nigel, Kay and Gilly got it, so why couldn't I get it? I just felt like an idiot for my lack of understanding. At the time, I knew nothing about mental health services. If I did, I would have gone to see someone.

Gilly and I went to marriage guidance counselling, but

it was a case of me not understanding that Gilly loved me, and that I would not listen to her, but I felt no one was listening to me. We talked to Graham Brown, the leader of Turning Point, but he just said that it takes time and that all relationships go through hard times. We needed to love and trust each other, which was true, but love and trust could not stop my paranoia.

Gilly and I talked a lot but it never helped my mental health much. I loved Gilly more than anything, but my mind let me down; my mind was the problem. Around this time,I got some work from my brother doing some labouring work. It was a Saturday and I drove to the job, which meant I had to drive down the motorway, which was no problem. I arrived at the job on time and parked the car. My brother was talking to a guy so I just stood and waited for him to tell me where to go. They were laughing and joking, which made me feel uneasy. I felt that they were laughing at me and, because I was so paranoid, my mind was racing. My thoughts were confusing … I believed Gilly was having an affair. My mind was locked in turmoil and, during the morning I was there, I started to think the people I was working with were trying to set me up. I saw a guy who looked like me and immediately believed I was being set up. There was no doubt about it. The first chance I got to leave, I did. I drove home down the motorway, thinking I was being followed. I drove the car behind lorries or to the side to stop the cameras from following me. My mind was focused on getting home to find Gilly with the police who were going to arrest me for stealing from the job. I was convinced and very paranoid. My mind was racing with hundreds of thoughts – everyone hated me and Gilly was only with me to hurt me.

When I reached the house, I came through the house by the kitchen door. As I came in, I locked the door behind me and then locked the front door. Gilly asked me why I was home so early.

"You know why," I replied. I kept going to the windows to see if the police were coming. I was on edge, pacing the floor. After about half an hour, Gilly asked me if I wanted to take the dog for a walk.

"Yes," I said. Anything to get out of the house. I was highly sensitive and deeply troubled. We drove to a local beauty spot and walked Roy, the dog. During our time there, a helicopter hovered over our heads. I thought that this was the police following me and I hid behind trees until they left. My heart was racing, my mind in a dark place. I was convinced the whole world was against me. We got back to the house and, again, I locked all the doors. Gilly kept asking me what was wrong.

"You know what's wrong," I said. I started to think the TV and video had a hidden camera, filming me. We didn't talk very much all afternoon.

At some point, Gilly phoned her friend to say we were not

GERALD O'DOWD

going over to their house and Gilly went to bed a few hours later. I lay on the sofa, going over in my mind how everyone was trying to set me up. I put the radio on because I believed the TV and video were filming me. My mind raced with so many thoughts. At some point, I went to bed thinking about how my wife and the world hated me. During the night, I lost all control of my senses. At this point, I feel the details should be kept to myself because I don't want to hurt or bring back bad memories to Gilly's mum, dad, brother Graham, family and friends.

Gilly shouted at me to get out of the house, which I did. I walked to the police station. I was a babbling mess, talking nonsense. The police officer asked me questions, but I was not making any sense. It is hazy from then onwards and I was heartbroken, confused and lost in grief. My lawyer and brother were outside the room by now and, at some point, a psychiatrist came to see me. He was very indifferent towards me – cold, detached and not very friendly. I was still feeling deeply paranoid.

My brother was deeply concerned about my welfare and treatment. The police were kind towards me and my lawyer was very sensitive with me. I felt lost, confused, deeply sorry and troubled with what I had done. I could not believe my actions. I was shocked. That night, I was kept in the cells and, in the morning, I was taken to Woodhill Prison in Milton Keynes. All the prisoners, including me, had a shower before being taken to our cells. I was taken to the hospital wing where I was given my prison uniform – a new shirt, trousers and black plimsolls. The other prisoners were friendly and the staff were kind. I was lost in my own world; confused, anxious and paranoid. My solicitor came to see me, but I thought he was trying to play games with me. He seemed very kind, but could I trust this man? If I am honest, I did not trust a soul and my mind was all over the place. I cried and had no appetite or strength. I lay on my bed and could not move. One night, a big guy came over to me and hugged me. He said that he understood my pain. The staff were kind to me, but I did not talk much to anyone. The doctor put me on anti-depressants, which did not do much for my paranoia. The weeks went by and my family visited me every day, which was a huge comfort to me. They took it in turns to visit me – my parents, my brothers and sister came to my rescue, even though my mind was filled with paranoia, I felt the pain in them.

My mum told me that Tracy, Lisa, Ann and Fiona had all phoned my mum to say they could not believe what I had done because it was not in my nature. Over my time locked up, they all came to see me, which was also very comforting. The last time I saw Tracy, she was pregnant with her first child. I hope she is well and in a great relationship; in fact, I wish all my exes love and happiness. I thank them for their generosity of heart coming to see me at my darkest moment. This book is about the power of love, the love of my family, friends and the authorities, the prison staff, doctors, psychiatrists, therapists, mum, dad, brothers, sister, uncles, aunties, cousins, all my family, my CPN, care plan nurse Frances, who took over my care when I left hospital and who is now a good friend. We meet up regularly and talk often. She is an angel and looked after me at a low point in my life.

After a few weeks in prison, the staff told me a psychiatrist was coming to see me. On the day he came, I was on my bed sleeping. The psychiatrist was very matter of fact, a little cold and distant and not very warm. He asked me about the days leading up to the incident with my wife Gilly, and how I was feeling in the months before. He was with me for about an hour. After he left, I went back to my bed to sleep. I was getting more depressed day by day, sleeping was becoming my way of life. When I was sleeping, I wasn't thinking about my wife. I loved my wife deeply and couldn't come to terms with what I had done. They were dark times and all I could think about was Gilly, her mum and dad, brother, family and friends. I hated myself more than ever, and sleeping was the only way to not consciously think about my wife.

All I could do was sleep. I couldn't eat and lost my will to live. Every day, I thought about suicide, which was impossible as I was being watched twenty four hours a day. The wardens were kind, the other prisoners were kind, my family was amazing, but my mind was paranoid. I could not trust anyone – that's why I could not eat or drink anything because I believed they would poison me. I was lost in darkness, which was not being supported in prison. They gave me anti-depressants but I needed stronger anti-psychotic drugs. After six weeks in prison, I travelled to the hospital with two guards and a driver. We arrived in daylight and all the doors were locked, and I remember hearing keys jangling when nurses walked by. We went through several doors before we got to my ward. I was taken to my new bedroom where I put my things. I felt anxious, paranoid and very frightened; this was a secure mental health institution, housing very dangerous and broken people. My mind was working overtime. I was given an injection of an anti-psychotic drug, which didn't seem to work at first. I felt strange in my new world. I walked down the hallway and a guy punched another guy full in the face; then another guy set fire to a newspaper in the TV room. A short time later the TV was thrown against the wall over an argument about what to watch.

My first day was interesting and volatile: a measure of things to come. I spent most of the time sleeping. It took two weeks for the injections to take hold and, when it did, I was unplugged from the mains – the lights were on but I was not home anymore. I slept even more, which was okay with the staff. I didn't mix that well at first, but as time went by, I made friends. In fact, I got on with everyone. I spent most of my time listening to music, watching TV or playing pool. Life was okay at the hospital and I settled into life there. In all my time there, I never had a bad word with anyone, staff or patients. The medication was powerful, which slowed me down, but the place was home for the next several years. The first year, I spent sleeping. Some days, I could not get my head off the pillow. I was deeply depressed and I cried most nights in my room and constantly beat myself up. I felt deep sorrow and guilt; I felt I had ruined Gilly's family's life and my family's also. I had ruined everything. My son came to see me, but they were not normal meetings because there was always staff with us. My spirit was dead and I had constant thoughts of suicide. I felt that, if I was dead, everyone would be better off – my son, my parents my brothers and sister. I was lost in a sea of despair and self-loathing. My son was constantly on my mind; I had ruined his life and he was five years old. Gilly loved him and he loved her. Suicide was the only way out of this nightmare. I loved my son deeply and believed he would be better off without me. My mum kept telling me to pray and stay positive. Mum was my rock, and my hero. In the darkness, she was the light that kept me going. Every Friday, my mum and sister Siobhan came to see me. The visits made life worth living. Most times, my friends in the hospital would sit with us for a chat. I looked forward to seeing them so much.

One time, a fight started while they were with me. It was

over a stolen watch. I was anxious, more for my mum and sister, but it was soon over. Violence erupted many times over the years. On another occasion, a guy threw boiling hot water into another patient's face, causing burns to his face and chest. But the worst incident happened one evening, when a guy gauged out another patient's eyes with his bare hands, and then bit off his big toe. The staff tried to cover it up but we saw the guy being walked around the hospital grounds a week later. I kept my room locked at night while I was sleeping. It was a dark place to be. One guy kept setting fire to his bedroom. I was offered drugs and alcohol, which was readily available at a price. Like in all institutions, you could get anything you wanted within reason. People were smoking weed, but I never touched anything because I was paranoid about being more paranoid. Some of the girls self-harmed, and one in particular slashed her throat with a broken cup. She had scars all over her arms. She was a sweet girl who was abused from a young child. One day, one of the girls went into the shower with a guy who basically used her for sex. He was bragging about it for a week. I could not stand the guy, he was a slimy and cunning prat. No one said anything but I never trusted him with anything.

On another occasion, a girl cried rape after accusing a guy, but she retracted the next day. The place was full of broken people and it affected me emotionally and mentally. I spent a lot of time in my room listening to music, praying or writing songs and poetry. This was a great channel for getting my emotions out. After my first year, I started to do group work, like playing football, badminton, group therapy, talking in a group with my peers, and the thing that helped me most was art therapy. This was a huge shift in my ability to mix better and bring out my dark thoughts of suicide. I never spoke about my suicidal feelings to anyone, but it was a constant in my thoughts and feelings. My self-esteem was at an all-time low, my confidence was non-existence and I was lost in my dark thoughts. I should have opened up but felt trapped in my head. No one asked so it never came up. I found it very difficult to talk in a group, but art therapy was great for me. I looked forward to going there and being creative helped my mental state for a short time. Any time spent outside my room, I was with my mate who also loved music and art. We talked and drunk tea. My mate was a chatterbox and a lovely guy, plus he is a good artist who I hope will keep doing it.

Life on the ward was boring at times, with nothing to do most of the time. On weekends, nothing happened. The staff had the weekend off so we had to make do with our own company; no groups and a skeleton staff. If you had a visit, it was something to look forward to. My ex-girlfriends came to see me, Tracy, Ann, Fiona and Lisa. We chatted but I had nothing much to say; I felt ashamed of how I had become so mentally ill when they had all moved on with their lives and were in new relationships. It made me feel a little better that they had moved on and that we could still be on friendly terms. I hope that's still the case.

The hospital chaplain came in to see us some weekends. It was good to pray with him and chat about what was troubling us. He told me I was a good man that had done a bad thing, which helped me a little. Prayer was important to me and, every day, I prayed for Gilly and all her family, my family, my friends and the whole planet. Shine your light on everyone, Lord. Give them peace in their hearts and minds, show them your loving light, Lord. Love them and look after them, now and always. Bring them happiness and peace; heal them with your deep love. Amen.

I asked for forgiveness every day and spent most days beating myself up. I just could not come to terms with what I had done. I kept saying I am so sorry to Gilly; I saw her image in my mind all the time. I rarely say what's on my mind, even now I say very little. I am getting better at talking but I am a private person. I understand people's scepticism and I understand people's misgivings. Some people have blanked me, some are rude, some are indifferent. People have made up stories that are fictional bullshit. People make up shit when you're on your knees; they pick on weak, vulnerable, defenceless people. Because I was so mentally ill, I couldn't talk. I suffered because I could not communicate properly. In hospital, everyone was in the same boat, so I never suffered mental bullying there. I am very intuitive and I know when someone is being real or not. I have lost touch with many people over the years and many friends have left my life – that makes me sad. The only people I can truly trust are my family.

They understand the struggle and they don't judge me. I can be myself without feeling shit about life. Hospital life was okay; I joined groups, gardening, picture framing, even going out of the hospital to do small decorating jobs for people for free. The years went by and life was normal in hospital. It was life inside an institution. I had my own room where I could escape people, when I was feeling down or emotional. My family made life worth living. My mate Ricky and his girlfriend Sarah visited me, which was great. Ricky is one of the most nicest people you will ever meet. Also, my mates Mick, Gus, John and Ann Marie came to see me with my brother Richard. I was lucky – most patients had no one. That's why I never went back to the hospital; it was the saddest place on earth, full of broken hearts and souls.

I feel bad for not returning but I suffered from acute anxiety/panic Attacks. These started when I got my first freedom from hospital, on a day out to be with my son. He was visiting London Zoo with his cub's group. I met them at Charing Cross train station. I was nervous but excited to see and be with my son. The day was great, Joseph, who was then about five years old, the people and children were friendly and it was a great experience until we were traveling back to Charing Cross on the underground. The tube was packed with commuters and this feeling of complete dread came over me. My heart started beating fast and I could not breathe properly. I felt I was losing control of my mind. I made my excuse and got off at the next station. I ran out of the station into the fresh air, my heart pounding. I paced up and down the street, trying to be as normal as possible. It must have looked a little weird and strange, but I was so in the panic, I didn't notice. After what seemed ages, my heart slowed down and I started to feel a little bit better. I think it lasted around thirty minutes but it felt like a day, and when I got back to the hospital, I was glad to be back in my room safe.

I felt these panic attacks would stop the psychiatrist from letting me go home, so I kept quiet about them. My main aim now was being with my son. I hated the fact that he could not see me unchaperoned and I wanted to make up for leaving him and ruining his young life. I felt deeply ashamed for not being a good father. I was lost in a sea of pain and confusion over my son and I so wanted to make it up to him.

One day, when I was on the ward, a lovely lady nurse, who I played scrabble with, came to see me to tell me I was going to the flats. I was really shocked that I was on my way out of hospital. I thought she was joking, but she was not. She told me to bag up my belongings and report to the nurse station. We walked from the ward to the flats where I was shown to my new room. It was called 'the flats' but it was really a shared hostel type of set up. There were four of us sharing the cooking, cleaning and living room. We all had our own bedrooms, which was cool with me. The other guys were great and we all got on okay. I spent twelve weeks in the flats before getting the message that I was leaving for home. Over the last year, I had tribunals with a judge who decided I was safe to go home. My psychiatrist was happy that I was not a danger to people or society and I was happy to go home, but the panic attacks were really getting strong and I felt scared and emotional, which stopped me being happy.

My brothers Rich and Kev picked me up in a rented van, which was bittersweet; I was leaving my mates and all the other guys and girls. I felt guilty for leaving them behind, but was glad to see my family, so I had mixed emotions. Rich and Kev were great fun and they made me smile for the first time in ages. I was moving to a hostel in SE18, near to my family, which was great. My son came to visit me and played pool and darts. I took him swimming and to football. He was growing up fast and I had missed three years of his life so I wanted to make up for the lost time. Joseph was a good football player and played for a local team called the Robins. When I got my driving licence back, I drove him to his matches all over South London. It was nice to be his dad again, but the panic attacks got worse. On several occasions, I had major attacks while watching him play, which made it very difficult to mix with the other mums and dads. I managed to get by but I must have been a little strange to them. I was trapped in my head, feeling useless and unworthy, feeling not good enough. I thought everyone was judging me but they were unaware of my mental state. In hindsight, they probably did not even think about it. To them, I was just a quiet guy. The reality was, I hated myself, but no one knew how I was feeling because I never spoke about it.

Around this time, I had counselling at Mind in Greenwich, which helped me a little. I also joined a therapy group for men at Mind, which was also very useful, but the panic attacks continued to cripple my confidence. During my son's end of season football presentation night, I had a massive panic attack and had to leave early. Again, I felt like I had let my son down. I can't put it into words other than it felt like I was losing my mind and control of my life. They were horrible, nasty reminders of my mental health problems. My medication was so strong that I was still sleeping a lot and had no get up and go. I could not talk very much; I was numb and depressed, feeling like a loser in life. I felt my life was not worth living and suicide filled my thoughts. I was a useless father, a shell of the man I used to be, the days of football, boxing running marathons and triathlons was another lifetime away and I could not not function in the real world.

My family and friends helped me so much but my mind stopped me from truly loving myself and life. I was trapped in my thoughts of suicide and being unworthy. My family was my shelter from the darkest moments. Life was harder on the outside and I judged myself harshly when everyone showed me great compassion and love.

My son had a football five-a-side tournament in Norfolk, which my mum, sister, aunty, uncle and son went to. We stayed in a caravan which was very Spacious. We had been there for a few hours when I had a massive panic attack in the caravan. I tried to lay down but it got worse. The caravan spun around and my heart was beating so fast that I thought I was going to have a heart attack and die. I managed to get through the weekend but it was very hard. This went on for years.

My CPN found a group that helped me to manage my attacks. The people were really supportive and kind and the group helped me to overcome the stigma attached to anxiety disorders. I was scared of my own shadow and full of fear. My psychiatrist gave me diazepam to help me cope with going out. She told me not to take them all the time, only when I was in a real panic. Just having them helped me greatly. The panic attacks stopped me from going out. On New Year's Eve 1999, the most anticipated New Year's Eve celebrating the new millennium, I spent the evening in the grip of a massive panic attack, lasting most of the night. My life was a nightmare every day, fearing another attack. My family were gentle with me and this went on until around 2003 when they stopped without warning. They left as strangely as they arrived, with no conscious thoughts.

I felt God was punishing me for my past and I felt that I deserved to be punished. Self-loathing was my friend; it controlled me for many years. How could I love myself when I had committed such a heinous crime? How could I move on from such a massive event? I felt I could not move on with such a dark tragedy in my mind, heart and soul. I was stuck in the bottom of a dirty, dingy, dark barrel, slashing around in my guilt, pain and deep sorrow. I kept saying sorry to God for my actions. It was in 2003 that I made a decision to end my life. I was so down and felt useless. I put every pill I could find in a cereal bowl, I opened a bottle of vodka and took the pills. I lay on my bed feeling death would be the answer. I am not sure how long I was on the bed before my sister shouted through my letterbox. I was very disorientated and fuzzy, and I am not sure what she said, but I managed to get off the bed and crawl to the front door. I opened it and collapsed on the floor. My brother Kevin lifted me onto his shoulders and took me down to my sister's car. I was unconscious and don't remember anything. My sister saved my life that night, for sure. I was taken to the local hospital where they pumped my stomach. I spent two days in the general hospital before being put into the local psychiatric hospital up the road. Again, my family came to my aid, visiting me, supporting me, loving me. My Aunty Teresa and Uncle Barry came down from Birmingham, my mum and sister visited me, my brothers gathered by my side. There is no power greater than love.

Again, love saved me from death. My sister is an amazing sister with two beautiful childrenl she is my hero and I owe her my life. While I was in hospital, the psychiatrist changed my depression medication from an injection to a drug called Sertraline and an anti-psychotic pill called Olanzapine. After two weeks of being on them, my mental health took a massive turn for the better. These drugs changed my life and, mentally, I felt better than ever.

My mental health became more and more on an even keel, more equilibrium, more normal. I tried several times to stop my medication but each time I fell into a deep depression, anxious and paranoid. Now, I exercise often, eat well and take my medication, which makes my life more fulfilling and wonderful. My mental health is good to excellent and my relationships are much more rewarding and loving. Meditation also brings clarity and peace, things fall into place more easily with love in your life and affirmations help the healing process, but having Louise L Hay in my life was a game changer.

One Saturday, I went to a body, mind and spirit weekend and found a stall with flyers on it for Louise L Hay workshops run by a lovely lady called Daphne. There was no one on the stall but that flyer changed my life, by chance, luck or fate. It was divine intervention picking up that flyer. It started my journey into the work and philosophy of Louise L Hay. Daphne helped me with love and kindness, she lived the teachings and is a wise and intelligent tutor of 'you can heal your life' workshops. We became good friends and I completed several workshops and meditation course. Daphne took part in a long walk for peace and we trained together for it, which got me back into doing more exercise.

Also, Daphne recorded a CD and asked me to paint her a painting as the cover, which was exciting and nerve racking at the same time. I did three paintings and she loved one enough to use it; that made me feel great and boosted my confidence. In 2003, I decided to do a college art and design foundation course at Bexley College, which surprised me when I got excepted. The course was very diverse, including photography, drawing, painting and digital manipulation using photoshop and sculpture. The year flew by and, during the year, one of the tutors asked me about going to university, which blew me away. I had never dreamed of doing that, so I gave it a go and, to my astonishment, got an unconditional offer from East London University. The icing on the cake was gaining a distinction for my foundation year. I must say a big thank you to all the tutors on the course and my fellow students. I hope everyone is doing well and enjoying life.

In 2005, I started my BA Degree at East London Docklands campus, which was testing but very worthwhile and mind expanding. I got some help from the disability advisor with a new laptop computer, which helped me tremendously with my course work essays and my general day-to-day learning experience. The course was very diverse with an open-minded approach to the artwork we produced. We had several tutors and workshop places, including printmaking, sculpture, painting, photography, film and drawing. We were expected to try new approaches and ways of creating our art practice and we had to talk in groups about our work and expand our knowledge of artists and their work. The course really opened my mind to trying new ways of thinking and making art. We went to art galleries all over London and read extensively about famous and not so famous artists, which made me want to do more experimental artwork by thinking outside the box and being open to criticism and other students' and tutors' opinions. We went to presentations by visiting artists, including the very open and funny Grayson Perry who was very interesting and knowledgeable. I got into current and up-and-coming artists and studied like mad. At times, it got over whelming and difficult, but during my time at East London University, I enjoyed mixing with first, second and third year students and the diversity of their artwork. It was mind expanding and exciting to be part of that journey.

In 2008, I graduated with a 2.1 BA honours degree in Fine Art, which was incredible as I had left school with no qualifications. I felt proud for achieving that degree – it was very satisfying. After university, I showed my art in several shows all over London, I entered several competitions and had my work featured in a few magazines.

In 2012, I went back to East London University to complete a master's degree in Fine Art, which was exciting and very scary at the same time. I found myself eager to learn, which was a good thing for me. My tutor, Grenville Davey, who won the Turner Prize in the '90s, was a great teacher and mentor to all his students. He helped me to grow as an artist and as a person. He was tough and gritty, but genuine and honest, making us question our integrity as artists. He was good at curating and passing on his wisdom to us, always willing to help us in any way possible. At one point, I felt like quitting, but Grenville helped me to see the bigger picture and move forward, which I think speaks volumes about his character and leadership skills. We took part in several exhibitions on campus and other venues and galleries around London. They were great experiences and good fun, and all the students got on well, which was great for all of us. Our graduation exhibition was fab and great fun, and my family came along. We finished the course in June 2014 and I passed, which was a great tonic for my confidence. I wish Grenville, all the teaching staff and all my fellow students the very best for the future. I thank them for the kindness and generosity of heart. I wish it had never finished, but everything does so build a bridge and get over it, as my Aunty Phill says.

Since leaving university, I have exhibited my work in many exhibitions around London, including with my dear friends Steve and Caroline Honest who run a vegan-friendly shoe showroom in the East End. I love going to galleries with my partner, Jo. She loves art too but doesn't like pretentious artists, who will remain confidential. I have submitted a book of artwork and poetry to a lovely publishers in London and am waiting for a reply. My recent work is going well. Making art is my therapy and it helps me to feel calm and inspires me to be the best I can be as an artist and as a human being. Art can transform your thinking, making life interesting and exciting. I love being creative: song-writing, poetry, painting, sculpting, singing, drawing, photography, short films. Being creative helps with my mental health problems. My journey has been tough, with all the sporting achievements, running marathons, the Ironman Triathlon, the toughest race in the world, the Fosters Quadrathon and boxing are nothing compared to dealing with mental health issues. Depression is tough on its own, but dealing with depression, anxiety, panic attacks, paranoid psychosis and no confidence or self-worth is hard. My life has been transformed by the philosophy and work of Louise L Hay.

In 2016, I completed the 'you can heal your life' teaching programme in Birmingham with an amazing group of people from all walks of life. Our teachers were fantastic and it was the best week in my life. The love and friendship was pure, natural and totally honest. We had the best teachers and venue. There was pure love with the most positive feelings. I let the love in with no fear or negativity, and it was genuine love with no judging each other. Since doing the course, I meditate most days and do mirror work with positive affirmations. I use tapping therapy, eat well, exercise most days, go swimming, walking and work out at the gym. I am looking for a good yoga class and I have studied at the world spiritual university with the Brahma Kumaris at Global Co-operation House in Willesden Green, learning yoga, meditation and positive thinking. I go to the men's spirituality group on a casual basis. I spent a lovely weekend at their Oxford retreat centre; it was a beautiful experience they are free regardless of wealth or position in life. It is free to attend workshops and courses. If you're looking for a peaceful place to learn and grow, they are the perfect organisation.

In 2009, I started a relationship with my partner, Jo. We have known each other for over twenty years, but only got together after being single for five years. We get on well most of the time and Jo makes me laugh everyday. She is very honest with her love. Jo has travelled the world, dancing in the Brazil carnival, driving through Costa Rica with her mad mate, living in Holland and Spain. Jo has always been independent and a free spirit; she loves life and danced most weekends all over the world. She is no wallflower and always speaks her mind. Jo has helped me to overcome my fear and anxiety, and we laugh most days, which has been a great tonic. She has stuck by me, despite my mental health issues and I feel nothing but love for her. Jo had a kidney transplant in 2011, which was very successful, but unfortunately, she had a major stroke a few years later, losing the use of her left hand side, paralysing her left arm and leg. She gets frustrated and has anger issues, which is normal for people who have had strokes. I am her full time carer now, which is fine by me, and we are very happy.

My journey has just begun. I am committed to the philosophies of Louise L Hay's work; I am committed to teaching the workshops and using the tools to help people live more fulfilling lives. For me, it has only just started and I understand it will be a lifetime's work, undoing my limitations, learning to love unconditionally, dealing with my years of negative thinking, trusting that life will work out, but it starts with me – no one else. I except my own negative past and look to the future with hope and love. I pray every morning and every night with gratitude and humble love. In the past, I worked hard on my physical body but neglected my emotional and spiritual values; today, I work hard on every aspect of my mind, body and soul. I read books on spirituality, personal development and self-help publications. My mum has been a great role model; she has a very strong faith and she is my teacher and inspiration. Mum is a mentor without even knowing it. She has a great work ethic and has a great moral code. It is never too late to change the direction of your life, however dark, however mixed up, however complicated. You can heal your life and you can change your life.

I recommend reading Louise L Hay's books and all the teachers in personal development. Hay House is a good place to start; look them up on the internet. From the time I did my first 'you can heal your life' workshop with Daphne in 2003, my life has grown immeasurably; my mind is clearer on the right path to follow. I do learning courses all the time because we never stop learning, I have become a life time learner, every year I do a course to develop my mind, keeping my mind active reading and watching positive films and documentaries. Jo and I go to art exhibitions as often as possible. Although I don't see my friends much these days, they are always in my mind; we had some great times growing up, but my priority now is my partner, Jo. Being a full time carer is hard and time consuming, my friends will always be my friends and always in my heart, but now I am looking after Jo 100%. I hope people understand, but, if they don't, I am sorry/ I would not judge anyone for their beliefs or moral stance.

Jo is vulnerable and needs help with most things: cooking, cleaning, hospital visits, dressing and food shopping. I like looking after her and being a carer has come naturally to me. We have our own interests, which is healthy. Jo has great friends and family who look out for her; her brother lets us stay at his house in Spain for a few weeks each year/ We go and see her dad most weeks. He is 83 now but in great shape. I see my mum every week; my son lives with his girlfriend and is totally self-sufficient. We talk every now and then. I wish we could see more of each other, but he is an independent man with a busy life and he does his own thing which, as a parent, is double-edged. You want your kids to be self-sufficient but miss them like crazy when they don't call you. That's life. I love Joseph with all my heart and wish nothing but the best for him.

Children have to make their own mistakes and triumphs, I hope he knows I will always love him and I am always here for him, whatever happens in his life, good or bad. My dad was an angry man who found it difficult to be gentle, but I know he loved me in his own way and he was my biggest teacher, good and bad. I miss my dad and truly believe he could have been a great teacher had he grown up in different times with more opportunity. He was as bright as a button, but was a hopeless gambler with many insecurities which he passed onto us kids. He did the best he could with little understanding of love, trust and gentleness. I loved my dad, warts and all, and I know he loved me, warts and all. I am not looking for perfection, I just want to be the best person I can be. Like my dad, I have insecurities and faults but I am committed to do better, be better, each and every day. If people don't like me, then that's their problem, not mine. I like me and I love me for who I have become. I made many mistakes, went down many wrong roads, listened to the wrong people, but I can say that I have worked very hard to change my thinking, as well as learn from my failures. Living with regret or anger won't help any situation. I can honestly say that I don't hate anyone or anything. Life is what you make it and karma will find you no matter what. I feel no animosity towards anyone who hurt me, and I hope no one feels that way about me. I love my family and friends, old and new. The people who spiked my drink with LSD are cowards who know nothing about love, but I wish them well. The dark side of that drug are well documented.

Syd Barrett of 60s' group Pink Floyd became mentally ill by using LSD and lived like a hermit for many years; he never recovered and died some time back. Peter Green of super group Fleetwood Mac took LSD at a party at a commune in Munich, Germany, and never recovered. People who spike drinks with LSD are cowards who laugh at seeing people suffer. Ben Fogle, TV and radio star, had his drink spiked with LSD and had a nightmare experience. His wife watched him have a full psychotic meltdown. Ben said that the experience was the worst of his life, and only his wife saved his life. He said that he can't forgive the person who spiked his drink. The only way to describe the feelings of an LSD trip is pure darkness, pure paranoid hell. It is no joke, it is far from funny, but the people who do this kind of thing are hateful and mindless, who lead sad lives; watching someone suffer is cold, dark and insensitive. I hope this kind of thing is stamped out. I hope no one has to go through that kind of experience ever again,

The effects of MDMA / ecstasy and potential acute adverse health effects: marked rise in body temperature (hyperthermia), dehydration, electrolyte (sodium) imbalance, high blood pressure (hypertension), involuntary jaw clenching and teeth grinding, muscle or joint stiffness, lack of appetite, illogical or disorganised thoughts, restless legs, nausea, hot flashes or chills, headache, sweating, faintness, panic attacks, loss of consciousness, seizures, kidney failure, swelling of the brain.

Longer term health effects: arrhythmia (irregular heartbeat) and heart damage, irritability, depression, impulsivity, impaired attention and memory, anxiety, aggression, sleep disturbances, concentration difficulties, lack of appetite, heart disease, decreased cognitive function.

The truth about cocaine and short term effects of cocaine:

Cocaine causes a short lived, intense high that is immediately followed by the opposite intense depression, edginess and a craving for more of the drug. People who use it often don't eat or sleep properly and they can experience greatly increased heartrate, muscle spasms and convulsions. The drug can make people feel paranoid, angry, hostile and anxious, even when they are not high. Regardless of how much of the drug is used or how frequently, cocaine increases the risk that the user will experience a heart attack, stroke, seizure, or respiratory (breathing) failure, any of which can result in sudden death.

Long term effects of cocaine.

A person can become psychotic and begin to experience hallucinations.

Coming down from the drug causes depression so severe that the person will do almost anything to get the drug, and if he or she can't get cocaine, the depression can get so intense, it can drive the addict to suicide.

Permanent damage to blood vessels of heart and brain, high blood pressure, leading to heart attacks, strokes and death, liver, kidney and lung damage, severe depression, and so on.

Drugs change your psyche; they damage you mentally, emotionally and spiritually. If you want to take drugs, that's your personal choice. Please think about your mental health before doing drugs that damage your mind and all your relationships. Very rarely do people come through unscathed. My idea about life is to help heal people with love, care and empathy. Louise L Hay was a master of love and inclusion, healing broken hearts and minds. In the 1980's, she worked with AIDS sufferers, helping them to love themselves while navigating the horrid disease HIV. She had hundreds of people coming to her workshops every week, learning that unity, love and peace were the way forward, and loving yourself so that you can love all of human kind, teaching that love is the greatest healer.

Music heals people and my brother George has helped millions of people with his songs. He is a prolific songwriter who is not interested in the business side of the record industry. He is a creative genius who shares his time helping other singers to make it. My brother David is a talented photographer; Kevin is a talented creative genius who gets bored easily. He designs clothes, paints and is a talented poet. Richard is a builder but could easily be a comedian; he is funny and interestingly intelligent. My sister has a great voice but hates singing in public; my grandad Glynn was a poet and used to make up songs for my mum and her siblings. My mum can make clothes, curtains, quilts, and she can decorate a house and create a wonderful garden. My dad was a photographer and had his own darkroom where he printed his photographs. My son Joseph is a talented artist, but doesn't pursue it in any way. Maybe when he gets older he will use his talent for drawing – only time will tell, I encourage everyone to try art of any kind. I write songs, poetry, I paint, sculpt, photograph, make small films and I love singing. We are a very creative family. All my mum's sisters can make clothes, knit, sew make all sorts of things out of material. My cousin Dominic can paint and sing; my cousin Dean is a genius music composer who has won several awards for his film scores. Art unites people and music concerts bring people together. Look at Live Aid and many other benefit gigs which support people all over the world.

I feel that politicians never look at the bigger picture regarding the future of mankind. They are taking our planet's resources without thinking of the future. They are now starting to do fracking in our country and deforestation in parts of the world are out of control. We need to wake up and save our planet and not look out for other planets to save human kind. Let's look after this one. We can do it if we become more empathic and care about the future of our children's children.

When we start on the path of spirituality, people are suspicious. They can't see the person now – they hark on about the past and our short falls. People do change and grow out of the chains of dysfunction and ignorance. I am looking at Buddhism, studying the principals and philosophy and my passion for learning is growing year on year. Every day is a blessing; all I have in my life is a major blessing. I am grateful for my family, near and far – my son is the greatest blessing; my partner, Jo, is a blessing; my pet Harry the cat is a lovely blessing. If we look around this wonderful, beautiful planet, there are blessings all over – the birds, bees, sunshine, oxygen, oceans, plants and trees, diversity of human kind, the animal kingdom on the land and in the sea. I am grateful beyond words. There are some very nice, decent people in all nationalities, creeds and genders. We all have much more in common than we think; unity and peace are closer than we feel.

This world universe creates enough wealth for everyone and there is no need for greed and hunger, no need for war's to obliterate this planet. Meditation can create humble serenity. My learning has brought me closer towards unity; when we let go of ego, let go of revenge, let go of judgment, let go, love your enemies, give your heart and soul to love, give your mind over to the light, grow from small mindedness, walk away from conflict, be the best that you can be in a loving excepting way. I want to serve and help people. I have faith we can do better as a people / human kind, and unite and be peaceful without drugs and alcohol. If we meditate every day and keep fit in body and mind, we can overcome racism, sexism, homophobia, ageism and we can be more mindful of each other.

My heroes are my mum, sister, brothers, son and all my family near and far – they have been incredible to me. I look to Martin Luther King, Gandhi, Jesus Christ, Buddha, John Lennon and Yoko Ono, Bob Marley and the Wailers, all men and women who stood up for love peace and unity. I listen to music that promotes unity, read books that teach peace. I listen to Martin Luther King's speeches to inspire me. Nothing happens instantly – it takes time and effort, mental, physical, spiritual and emotional. I catch myself being negative and change to a more positive vibe. I believe we can improve our life by keeping fit in body and mind, while being faithful to truth and honesty. The past is gone and we only have the now.

Louise L Hay was a visionary along with all the other visionaries, Jean Houston, John Assaraf, Rikka Zimmerman and endless seekers of the truth. My week with Patricia Crane and all the teaching team in 2016 was amazing. Learning to be a 'you can heal your life' teacher was the best thing I have ever done, life changing and very healing.

I needed to write my life story to hopefully inspire more men and women to open up to the philosophies of Louise's teaching. My dream is to become a great teacher. Some years ago, I was introduced to the YCHYL workshops and have not looked back; I met the most awesome people and shared a magical experience. Life is short; don't let it be too late for change. I love my son, mum, partner and family more deeply.

I reach for the light every day. My dad was wrong – fighting solves nothing. All it does is divide and separate people, and who cares how hard you can punch? I learned and acted out all my dad's ideas about being a man – men don't cry, men can't be vulnerable. All that utter bullshit is wrong; it is healthy for men to cry and feel their feelings. Being sensitive, caring and kind are a must if we are going to survive these crazy times. War is pointless, fighting is pointless, oppression and dominance is ugly. Growing up, our house was full of drama and tragedy, with early death from addiction to alcohol and drugs, screaming, shouting, crude language, no hugging, no kissing, no affection. These things are going on in houses all over the world – kids starving while parents argue over money, because the money went to the bookies or on drugs and alcohol or fags. The whole planet needs to wake up to love, peace and unity, not through mind-bending substances, but through caring, understanding, unity and inclusion. We are all in this together.

Over the years, different scenes have come and gone: mods and rockers, hippy times, the rave scene, built on a drugs culture. Uppers and downers, speed, coke, E, puff – we have tried it all over the years and still do. What if we could replace drugs with prayer, exercise, meditation, healthy eating, yoga, personal development courses and teach our kids that diversity, colour creed, sexuality and love are important lessons to learn. Why can't we teach kids these important life skills? It is a waste of time arguing, fighting or war mongering. When my dad lost at the bookies, he got angry and came home agitated, looking for a fight. We needed encouragement, gentle persuasion, love and hugs. No child asks to be born, and they arrive innocent and free from ego. This planet needs more people coming together; it's about we, not me. This planet is beautiful and freely giving, but it has its limits. Our children, their children and generations to come need us to be more thoughtful about how we treat and abuse this wonderful planet. We can all do something to help each other.

Volunteering is an excellent way to help the community. We are all in this together so why not start being more conscious about the way we act with everyone. If you can love your mother and father, you can love another human being, even if you don't know them personally. We are stronger together, united, not divided and isolated. The years I spent being mentally unwell have shown me that love can heal any problem. My mum, sister and family have shown me great love and understanding. At times, I felt suicidal and isolated, but my family were always there for me, whether it was talking or just listening, my family and the love they showed me helped to heal my mind. I love creating, whether it's song-writing, singing, painting, drawing, photography, sculpting, filming, poetry. It's my therapy and I enjoy creating. In feel at peace when I am creating, but love cured me from isolation, anxiety, paranoia and deep depression. I have many people to say a massive thank you to: my family, friends, doctors, psychiatrists, counsellors, my wonderful care plan nurse, Frances, my son Joseph for loving me and inspiring me to be a better man, to all the healers who worked their magic hands over my body and mind. I didn't get well on my own and it took the love of many people to bring me back to good mental, physical and spiritual health. You can heal your life with love.

Louise L Hay was a trailblazer, bringing love into our lives through her books and workshops. I am proud to be a 'you can heal your life' teacher; many blessings have I gained through her wonderful intelligence, grace and love. I thank God every day for bringing Louise into my life. Sadly, Louise passed away recently at the age of 90, which is very sad. The legacy left behind is so precious and life giving – my life and many other lives have been transformed by the philosophy and teachings of Louise L Hay and all the Hay House authors and workshop leaders. Thank you all the gentle souls who work tirelessly for the betterment of human kind. I am off to meditate now, full of gratitude and love for God's grace.

My mum, sister, brothers, dad, aunties and uncles, cousins, nieces, nephews and my nans and grandads have created a wonderful tapestry and family tree. I love the glue that keeps us all together and I love my family; we are all nuts and crackers, but in a good way. I have tried to be as honest as possible in this text but have left out certain details due to a sensitive nature. I feel no need to glorify or hurt anyone. This book tells my truth – highs, lows, twists and turns.

I loved my wife and think of her often. I feel sad about our short time together and wish I could turn back the clock and start again, but that's my sorrow. I wish her mum, dad, brother and wider family love and understanding. In my heart, I know I am a good person who did a bad thing. It is my wish to help human kind, support love and nurture anyone who needs my help. It has been hard at times with many tears, but I feel I can do good in the future, in Gilly's memory and in honour of my family, Gilly's family and the wider community. Teaching, giving loving, being a person that is professional, caring and honest in all my relationships.

Thank you for taking the time to read this book. I look forward to helping anyone who needs compassion love and understanding.

Love Gerald
'You can heal your life' teacher and student of life, Amen.

Depression

When i am down
Everything seems dark and hellish
People seem cold and distant
Life is not worth the living

When i am down
I sleep all day drifting out to sea
Darkness penetrates my mind
The sharks just want to savage

Me and my mind in deep despair
Im stuck in a rut going no where

When i am down
I need to take my pills
To keep me calm and clear
Through all the pain and fear

When i am down
The sun don't seem to shine
The moon is like the devil
Plotting how to fool me

Chorus

M8

Down down down
These feelings engulf my spirit
Down down down
No one seems to care

When i am down
Depression holds me like a vice
Panic seems to fill me
And love is like a stranger

Feels like no one cares

Love

Love is the master

of my soul

Love is

my eternal goal

Love is the wisdom

in my heart

Love is

the light that soothes my mind

Love my sisters

Love my peers

Love my brothers

Love my son

Love my mother & Father

Love is honest

Love is cool

Love is happy

Love is good

Love is the master of my soul

We Are One

I am fit
I am healthy
I am strong

I am unique
I am different
I do belong

I am love
You are love
We are strong

You are strength
You are beautiful
You do belong

In a world of ever changing ways
Where we fight for freedom everyday
We are one we are so beautiful
Stand united and we do believe

You are free
Open the door
You can fly

There's no limit
In your soul
There's enough for everyone

We must fight
For what is right
Say no to violence